ROARING
FAITH

COMPILED AND EDITED BY
DONNA SKELL

LISA B. WORLEY ◆ BELINDA MCBRIDE
FRANK BALL

Stories of Roaring Faith
Copyright © 2019 by Roaring Lambs Publishing

Published by:
Roaring Lambs Publishing
17110 Dallas Parkway, Suite 260
Dallas, TX 75248
Email: info@RoaringLambs.org

Dedication

To God,
Thank You for the difference
You make in our lives.

To Garry Kinder,
Founder of Roaring Lambs Ministries,
Because of you, this book is possible.

To all the contributors of this book,
Thank you for sharing your personal testimonies
With the world.

To all the readers,
May your relationship
With our Lord Jesus Christ grow.

Introduction

About thirty-five years ago, I had the opportunity to attend a small class that taught me how to confidently and effectively share the gospel against the backdrop of my life experiences. **It changed my life.** I learned the importance of sharing how God had proved Himself real to me.

Come and hear, all you who fear God; let me tell you what he has done for me. — Psalm 66:16

For the last several years, Roaring Lambs has been encouraging and equipping believers to effectively compose their testimony. Whether sharing one-on-one, speaking to a group, or just putting it in writing as a legacy for future generations, it is beneficial.

We will tell the next generation the praiseworthy deeds of the Lord, his power, and the wonders he has done, so the next generation would know them, even the children yet to be born, and they in turn would tell their children.
— Psalm 78:4, 6

Our testimony is our opportunity to let God use the circumstances He has allowed in our life for His glory. When you can take a difficult time, show how God used it for His good and yours, then you can give Him glory for that very hardship.

When he heard this, Jesus said, "This sickness will not end in death.

No, it is for God's glory so that God's Son may be glorified through it."
— John 11:4

Putting your faith story together will prepare you for many opportunities to share your faith. Each day, you are more likely to realize just how many there are.

But in your hearts revere Christ as Lord. Always be prepared to give an answer to everyone who asks you to give the reason for the hope that you have. But do this with gentleness and respect. — 1 Peter 3:15

The world needs to see how real Jesus is. Times are short. Your story matters. It is the living water that others need.

Then he said to his disciples, "The harvest is plentiful but the workers are few." — Matthew 9:37

Are you ready to be used by God and be richly blessed? Tell your story of what He has done for you.

Then I heard the voice of the Lord saying, "Whom shall I send and who will go for us?" And I said, "Here am I. Send me." — Isaiah 6:8

Donna Skell, Executive Director
Roaring Lambs

Acknowledgements

My sincere thanks are extended to Frank Ball for his gracious help turning this manuscript into a book. You are a kind, generous, God-loving man, and very appreciated by this ministry.

To Dan Thompson, our graphic designer from T-Bone Designs, many thanks for all your work with Roaring Lambs, to give us such a great look. You are talented and have established our visual image. Thanks especially for a great cover for this book.

Thank you, Sherry Ryan, for your work editing the testimonies. I know you were blessed by reading them, but we are blessed by all your spelling, punctuation, and grammar corrections.

To my co-compilers and editors, Belinda McBride and Lisa Burkhardt Worley, without the two of you, this book would have never been completed. Thank you for your endless hours of reading and re-reading the stories. Thank you for your attention to the small details.

Thank you, again, to all who contributed their personal testimonies. This book is not about you, but is all about our great and awesome God we serve.

Our Stories Shape Us

The importance of stories cannot be exaggerated, for they not only entertain but they also teach and edify. Ancient audiences recognized and revered the significant power of stories no less than we do today. Characters within some stories even embody the power of storytelling. Take, for instance, the Shaper in the ancient epic poem, *Beowulf*.

One of the most important stories in all of World Literature, *Beowulf* is an Anglo-Saxon narrative whose hero is Geatland King Hrothgar, lord of the Danes, a tribe living in the part of the world now called Denmark. Their enemies include the monstrous creature Grendel, a descendant of Cain, an outcast doomed to wander the face of the Earth.

One night, Grendel sees an old blind man enter the meadhall of Hrothgar's court. The man is a bard, a singing storyteller. Playing his harp, the Shaper entertains the Geat warriors with legends that edify, encourage, and embolden them, strengthening them for the perilous task of defending the kingdom.

In listening to the Shaper's stories, even the beast Grendel recognizes the real power of the Shaper, for he has the power to shape men and change the world. His stories about heroes, adventurous journeys, and noble accomplishments create wonder from apathy, order from chaos, meaning from confusion, and beauty from adversity. So do your stories!

Just as the Shaper promoted values and principles embraced by ancient peoples—heroism, compassion, love, and beauty—storytellers today wield the power of imagination to inspire people, raise their expectations of themselves, and change the world in which they live.

Shelley Allen, Roaring Lambs Director of Writing Services

Table of Contents

The Confession
by Kathleen Higgins

I looked into the face of the unknown priest, feeling relieved that he was young. I didn't know if an old man would understand my situation.

"Bless me, Father, for I have sinned. It's been a few years since my last confession."

The requisite words from the ritual of Confession flowed from my tense lips. I had never been to this church before, but I was in dire need of spiritual direction. I didn't trust my own judgment or even the counsel of a wise friend. I needed an expert. My life was unraveling, and the fate of my marriage depended on the wisdom of this unknown man of God.

I had met my husband, Jim, in a church basement in Moorestown, New Jersey, a couple of years earlier. He'd just moved to New Jersey to start a new job. He announced to my church group that he was single, from California, and that he arrived with just the clothes on his back. His boisterous laugh, sense of humor, and passion dominated the room. I was single and felt immediately drawn to him.

A year passed before we met each other again at a New Year's Eve party. There, we exchanged a New Year's Eve kiss. Several months later, we became movie buddies. After a spontaneous dinner trip to New York's Little Italy and an Easter dinner with my family, where Jim brought me white roses, we began dating.

I learned that Jim was separated, not single. He insisted that his marriage was over, and I wanted to believe him.

His wife had other ideas. She flew from California to Philadelphia to take care of his dog, Buddy, while he was scheduled to travel out of town on business.

I should have stepped aside, giving his marriage one last chance, but I was selfish and self-centered. Instead, I pushed forward with the relationship.

Jim's health was an immediate problem. He suffered from Type II diabetes and had recovered from a major stroke. The toes on his right foot became infected and had to be amputated.

1

Although he and I had only dated a few months, I visited him every day in the hospital and rehab. While he was home recovering at my condo, I changed his bandages. My mother didn't approve of my caretaking, but I couldn't abandon Jim in his time of need.

After he recovered and his job in Philadelphia was terminated, Jim found a job in Connecticut. We continued dating long-distance for several months. To push the relationship even further, I took an early retirement from my job as an assistant prosecutor in Camden, New Jersey, sold my condo, and planned to move in with Jim in Connecticut, where I would become a writer. That I was living in sin and breaking God's law never occurred to me. In this modern era, I saw "living together" as an interim step to marriage. The day I closed on my condo in New Jersey, the blood vessels in Jim's left eye hemorrhaged due to diabetes, blinding him and preventing him from driving or working. Instantly, I became Jim's driver and caretaker, which was not anything like I had planned.

Without Jim's income, living in Connecticut was too expensive, so we moved to League City, Texas, south of Houston, where Jim had an old friend. The weather was warmer, my pension wouldn't be taxed, and the cost of living was lower. Nevertheless, I decided to go back to work to make ends meet and found a job at the Galveston County probation office. I pushed Jim to divorce his wife, and then I begged for an engagement ring.

After a brief separation, Jim and I married on December 24, 2016, at the Venetian Hotel in Las Vegas. Jim was wearing a dark suit, white crisp shirt, gray tie, and a red rose boutonniere in his lapel. Neither Jim nor I could contain our joy. On a white wooden gondola, we held hands and declared our vows while traveling on the man-made canals of make-believe Venice. After the rented minister pronounced us husband and wife, the gondolier sang Italian love songs. Then he kissed me. The crowds lining up on the sides of the canal cheered. In my ivory sequined dress from Macy's and a cute bird-cage veil, I waved my bouquet of red roses like a royal queen in response.

A few months later in Webster, Texas, after seeing a movie at

2

the theater, Jim and I were eating barbecue at Bone Daddy's. As we dined on pulled pork, ribs, and potato salad, Jim contemplated the loss of his puppy, Jeffrey, yet again. Taking care of the energetic and playful puppy had helped Jim recover from his stroke in 2009. As a result, Jeffrey tugged at his heart more than any pet he had ever loved.

One evening, his grown stepson from his prior marriage left the yard gate unlocked at his house in Riverside, California. Jim had warned him repeatedly to lock the door. Jeffrey escaped and was killed by a passing vehicle. Jim loved his puppy so much that *Jeffrey* was tattooed on his chest. Jim blamed his stepson for Jeffrey's death and fantasized about his revenge in vivid, gory detail. His ruminating was killing him spiritually, inch-by-inch.

As Jim described his pain from the loss, I asked if he ever thought about what his stepson thought when Jim became his new dad and took over as head of household. Jim put down his fork and stopped chewing, visualizing his stepson's point of view for the first time. Suddenly, Jim realized that he had always treated his stepson like a loser and had constantly ridiculed him. He never thought about how his stepson must have felt when he lost his position in the family, when his relationship with his mother was interrupted.

At home when we were settled onto the leather sectional sofa in our living room, Jim pulled out his cell phone and composed an email. He asked his stepson for forgiveness for the way he had always mistreated him. He didn't mention Jeffrey. He was cleaning only *his* side of the street.

That made me think I needed forgiveness from one of my sisters for the way I always dismissed her. The more I resisted the idea, the more insistent the thought became. As I observed the growing freedom on Jim's face as he typed, I wanted that feeling too. I pulled out my cell phone and typed. After sending the email, I waited an excruciating ten minutes until I heard from her. She accepted my amends and said she had been waiting for it for a very long time. I was free.

After Jim and I sent our emails, we felt the power of God's presence. Peace and love filled our hearts. We cried with joy. God's Spirit filled the living room as we forgave and were forgiven. The physical room hadn't changed, but its essence transformed into a little slice of Heaven. Every resentment Jim had held against his parents, family members, and others evaporated. We broke free from the chains of resentment and unforgiveness that had shackled our spirits. For what seemed like hours that evening, we basked in His love.

The next morning, we were led to attend Mass for the first time in months. I wasn't a good Catholic. I avoided Mass because I found it dull. Today was different. After Saturday night's encounter with the Lord, every prayer and ritual was laced with new meaning. We wanted the feeling of God's presence to last as long as possible.

I awoke Monday morning with a powerful desire to get right with God regarding my marriage. Even though I was a non-practicing Catholic, that meant Confession. When I arrived at work, I met my supervisor, who was a Christian. Although I confided few details, my supervisor understood, and we agreed that I would take the day off.

Confessions were usually heard on Saturday afternoons, and it was Monday morning. I needed to find a priest willing to hear my confession immediately, before I lost my nerve. Did I have to make the biggest sacrifice of my life to get right with God? I understood that if God required me to make the sacrifice, I would have to follow through. There would be no choice.

I drove to a Catholic church in Texas City, about fifteen miles north of Galveston. I parked my car in the nearly empty lot and walked toward the building that had a cross on its roof. To my relief, the door was unlocked, and I entered. The sanctuary echoed with the clicking of my heels striking the floor. Bowing slightly toward the altar, I entered the wooden pew and sat down. I reflected on the question I was about to pose to the priest after my much needed confession. *Was there any other way, Lord?* I pulled down the cushioned kneeler, got on my knees, and clasped my hands, staring at the crucifix. I pondered my situation and prayed for a few minutes before getting up to find a priest.

I saw no priest in the church, so I exited the building and followed the sidewalk to the parish office. I opened the door and walked right into a man wearing a black shirt, black pants, and a white Roman collar. He was speaking to a woman in the hallway.

"Father, I need to make a confession."

The priest grasped the urgency of my situation and directed me to a conference room down the hall. As he closed the door, I fidgeted in my seat at the conference table.

"Bless me, Father," I said.

My need for Confession surprised me. The Bible says we are to "confess [our] sins to each other" (James 5:16). As a Catholic, confession meant a priest, even though my faith was shaky. Although I attended Mass occasionally, I was a cafeteria Catholic and did not accept all of the tenets of the faith. Now that I needed serious spiritual direction, I didn't know where else to turn.

Sitting across the table from the priest, I confessed my sin. Next, I needed to pose the big question: *Do I have to give up Jim?* Did God require me to sacrifice the one person I loved and who loved me? For three-and-a-half years in my twenties, I was married because I was afraid to be alone. After that, I was mostly single. Jim was my true love, and I was now fifty-four. If I lost Jim, I might be alone for the rest of my life. The Catholic Church did not permit remarriage after divorce. You had to obtain an annulment to remarry. Given these boundaries, I had no idea how this priest might direct me. Did Jim have to go back to his ex to be right with God? Would I have to take this step to remedy the damage I had done? Would that fix the past? Did I have to walk away?

"Do I have to leave my husband," I said, "so he can go back to his ex?" I studied the priest's face as he considered my question.

For a while, the priest said nothing. "No. You don't have to give him up."

I sighed as I let his words sink in. The tension in my body melted. In Genesis, Abraham offered his son, Isaac, as a sacrifice in obedience to God (Genesis 22:1-18). Before Abraham could strike Isaac, the Angel of the Lord appeared and advised him to spare his son. Abraham passed his test, and God honored Abraham's obedience. I was willing to give up the love of my life. I had passed my test.

The priest said, "I wonder how the Accuser will attack you."

I was taken aback. Most priests did not talk about the enemy and his attacks. Evil was more abstract. They preferred to talk about the love of Jesus. Only evangelicals worried about the enemy as a personal being.

"You mean the devil."

"Yes."

I had not considered what the devil might do in response to me reconciling with God. I had no idea what awaited me and was unprepared for the length and depth of his attacks. The priest gave no further words on how to prepare myself. Foolishly, I was not worried.

The priest pronounced my penance, and then he helped me with the words of the Act of Contrition, which I had forgotten. After he granted me absolution, I left the conference room, relieved and refreshed.

Having made my confession, I needed to make amends to Jim's ex, and so I drafted an email. I couldn't change the past, but I could humble myself, admit I was wrong, and ask forgiveness. I sent the email to Jim and asked him to forward the email to his ex when he felt the time was right. A few weeks later, she graciously accepted my amends.

Jim and I needed to find a church. I was reluctant to return to the Catholic Church since Jim didn't have an annulment. Not being married in the church might preclude us from receiving communion. Years earlier, I had attended a non-denominational, Spirit-filled church and was "saved." Jim had been raised Southern Baptist and was "rescued from his sin" as a teenager. He converted to Lutheranism in college and then became a Catholic as an older adult. I fondly remembered the Spirit-filled church I had attended. I thrived in the praise and worship and fellowship.

Jim asked a friend, whose spirituality we admired, what church he attended, and we were led to a non-denominational, Spirit-filled church in Dickinson, a town just south of League City. On April 30, 2017, we repeated the sinner's prayer together as we rededicated ourselves to Christ at the altar call.

Jim and I were hungry for the Word. We attended Bible studies and services on Wednesdays and Sundays, and a prayer meeting on Mondays. We prayed in bed every night and read from the Bible.

Shortly thereafter, I thought I should tell a certain defendant on my probation case list that God wanted him to know that *he mattered*. I recognized this thought was from the Lord. However, delivering this message risked my job because it would make me look crazy to people who didn't understand. Despite the cost, I had an overwhelming desire to obey the Lord. I found this man at his alcohol-drug outpatient rehabilitation center, looked him in the eye, and gave him the Lord's message.

One day, I thought about how no one knows how much time we have left on Earth. Any one of us could die on any day. The Second Coming of Jesus could happen today. Nothing was guaranteed. The Bible says "that day and hour no one knows, not even the angels in Heaven, nor the Son, but only the Father" (Matthew 24:36). With this in mind, I wanted one of my nieces to have a piece of jewelry that her deceased grandmother had left me. I sent Jim a text explaining this wish. He thought I was suicidal and called the police. Even though I arrived home safely, a few days later I was admitted to a mental hospital.

The enemy launched his attack, and he was not going to let go of me without a vigorous fight. I was hospitalized four times that year, suffering from delusions and paranoia. In my clearer moments, I wrote down scriptures on index cards and prayed them. When I didn't think I could fight any longer, I surrendered, and the Lord fought for me. The Bible says, "The Lord will fight for you; you need only to be still" (Exodus 14:14). The Lord was faithful and brought me through my battles for sanity.

We faced other trials and blessings in 2017. Jim had surgery and regained his eyesight in April/May. He searched for a job, but kept coming up short. We were frustrated, discouraged, and running out of money and credit. At the end of August, Hurricane Harvey clobbered Houston with fifty-two inches of rain. Our house accumulated eight inches of water. We evacuated our house and lived in shelters and then hotels for six months while our house was repaired. The Lord guided every step as we dealt with insurance adjusters and contractors. The Bible says, "Trust in the Lord with all your heart and lean not on your own understanding; in all your ways submit to him, and he will make your paths straight" (Proverbs 3:5–6).

Jim applied for jobs across the country with little luck. After another major job disappointment in November, he was ready to give up on job interviews and on God. With little hope, he interviewed for yet another job in Irving, Texas. This time, he nailed it. Although we had to move, we were staying in Texas. Answered prayer. The house was completed around the time Jim started his job in January/February 2018. We put the house on the market and received five offers in two days. The transaction was completed with only one minor hiccup.

We found a beautiful new apartment in Flower Mound, with a view of Lake Grapevine, ten minutes northwest of Irving. We googled churches and chose Heartland Family Church because we liked the name.

After the Parkland school shooting in Florida in February 2018, I felt led to start a ladies' prayer/Bible study in my home. The church agreed. We pray every Wednesday to protect the children in Irving and the Dallas Metroplex area. Then we pray however the Spirit leads. We conclude by studying the Bible over coffee and cake.

In November 2018, I started a blog about my journey and thoughts as a new believer. I am humbled that the Lord uses me to connect with believers and non-believers about my faith.

Despite all the trials in 2017, the Lord blessed us in 2018. I was freed from depression and anxiety. I didn't suffer any more delusions. I got the blues only two or three times, and I read scriptures and resisted the enemy until the mood lifted. Jim's diabetes is under control, and he is happy at work.

Today, I have joy, peace, and freedom. I pray, praise and worship God, and read the Bible. I have the knowledge and conviction that God has a plan for me (Jeremiah 29:11). I don't need to worry (Philippians 4:6). I just have to be willing to follow His direction. God knows my heart and He honors obedience and willingness. This can be challenging, since God has me on a "need to know" basis. He doesn't reveal His entire plan at once. There are many detours along the way. I know my life has a purpose, and He will guide me if I submit my will to Him.

Kathleen Higgins is a new believer and Christian writer. A retired Assistant Prosecutor from Camden, New Jersey, she currently writes a blog. She is a member of the Dallas Christian Writers Guild. She hosts a weekly ladies Bible study and prayer group at Heartland Family Church in Irving, Texas. She volunteers weekly at the Metroplex Women's Clinic in Arlington, Texas, where she provides spiritual counseling to pregnant women. Kathleen and her husband, Jim, reside in Lewisville, Texas. *MeTooForJesus.com.*

Thoughts to Ponder
from The Confession

1. Be willing to sacrifice what you love the most for the Lord.

2. Surrender your life to Christ and allow Him to fight your battles.

3. Submit to the Lord and He will direct your path.

What are you willing to sacrifice for the Lord?

"Do not lay a hand on the boy," he said. "Do not do anything to him. Now I know that you fear God, because you have not withheld from me your son, your only son." — Genesis 22:12

Finding the Real Prince Charming
by Jan Brand

It was happening again. I couldn't breathe, and my heart slammed against my rib cage. Was I dying? I was only twenty-four years old, and I wanted to live. As I stumbled next door and rang the doorbell, I tried to suck in enough air to breathe.

"Please help me." I gasped to get the words out around my fear. This was a new neighborhood, and I didn't know the neighbors, but my next-door neighbor got her car keys and purse and drove me to the nearest doctor's office.

When we approached, the receptionist's face reflected the same fear I felt. She jumped up, went through a door, and came back in seconds with the doctor, who led me to a treatment room. In a soothing voice, he asked questions as I wrung my hands and tried to keep fear at bay. All my senses were focused on the need to breathe, which was harder and harder, draining my energy.

After listening to different areas of my chest and back, the doctor sat on a stool and looked into my eyes. "You're having a severe panic attack. Can you tell me what's wrong?"

What was wrong? I was twenty-four years old, and life wasn't working for me. I had a sad, lonely childhood, and now I was married to a serial adulterer. I was the problem, because I couldn't make sense of life. Everyone knew the secret to happiness except me. I didn't want to live and die with nothing good in between.

I walked out of his office on trembling legs, with a handbag full of tranquilizers that were supposed to help me cope. However, they didn't work, because they couldn't make my husband faithful. They couldn't make me feel worthy of love, and they couldn't tell me life was full of promise, giving me hope for the future. The pills dulled the fear but did not help me be rid of the panic.

I soon found a way to diminish the severity of the attacks. I stayed in a safe place, my home, and I seldom ever left—not for the next ten years. Alcohol helped me relax better than the tranquilizers, so I ditched the pills and couldn't wait until five o'clock every day, when I deemed it acceptable to have a scotch and water.

At times, I felt strong enough to go to dinner with my husband and children. On a few occasions, I went shopping or attended something at one of the children's schools. But those occurrences were rare. For a decade, I was mostly housebound.

To the outside world, it looked like I lived the life of the privileged. The maid drove the children to school and did the shopping. A hairdresser came to the house to do my hair. And department stores sent saleswomen to my house, their cars loaded with clothes for me to try on in my bedroom. I didn't look like a candidate for an institution, but there was no doubt about it. People in psych wards were more in control than I was. I was a prisoner of terror in my own home.

When the attacks came, I lived inside a horror movie that wouldn't end. I tried counseling. After years of suffering, I would have talked to a monkey if I thought it could help. But regurgitating to a counselor the awfulness of my life only made my symptoms worse.

One bitterly cold winter day in desperation, I reached out to a woman I hardly knew. I had to find help. I couldn't go on. The president of my daughter's PTA had the reputation of being "religious." The few times we spoke at school, she seemed to have a sweet, gentle spirit, so I decided to risk it. I couldn't imagine that she belonged to a cult that threw you in the basement and screeched at you while beating you with glass-braided rope. Her family had been named "Family of the Year" by the *Lubbock Avalanche Journal* the previous year.

I called and asked if I could talk to her about school-related things. We made a date for two o'clock. I had learned to function with alcohol, so I tossed down two scotch-and-waters for courage and drove the four long, terrorizing blocks to her house.

The maid ushered me into a lovely home that smelled of oranges and cinnamon. Marilyn Nislar waited for me in the family room, and we settled onto a comfortable sofa before a roaring fire, where we drank spiced tea. As I looked around at the room filled with photographs and signs of love, I felt like weeping.

I didn't belong in this house. I wasn't sure I belonged anywhere, but I sure wasn't worthy to be here. But where else could I go? I didn't have a "get out of jail free" card, and with the hell I lived in—with daily panic attacks, heart pounding, gasping for air—I felt worse than being in jail. Life was hardly the happily-ever-after I had dreamed of as a child.

After a few minutes, I took a deep breath and decided to find out just what kind of Christian she was. I had nothing to lose. My life was out of control, and I couldn't fix it.

In a torrent of tears, I spilled out my story—the awfulness, the pain, the despair, the hopelessness, and the shameful secrets of my wild-child youth.

When I finished spewing my garbage into this idyllic setting and waited for her horrified response, she did an amazing thing. With tears sliding down her cheeks, she put her arms around me and said, "Oh, Jan, I always knew you were one of God's special kids. I just didn't know how special you were."

I was stunned. She thought I was special. Was it possible that God loved me? Wouldn't He count as someone Who cared, and did Marilyn really care too? This was heady stuff.

I didn't walk out of her house whole, but I walked out with a hope that began a wonderful change in my life. Sitting in her cozy family room, I saw Jesus, just like it was two thousand years ago, when He hung on a cross for me.

Ralph Waldo Emerson said, "Do the thing you fear, and the death of fear is certain." I began the process of recovery by leaving my safe place—my house. Hope is a funny thing. It gave me courage to try. Sometimes I hyperventilated the whole way, but I went.

I wasn't alone anymore. God cared, or so I had been told. Emerson said that if I did what I feared, it would go away. He was supposed to be a smart man, so his words had the weighty power of suggestion. I took tiny steps toward freedom. I felt that God stopped making worlds to reach down and rescue me. It didn't matter to Him if I was in a church or a velvet-lined gutter. He wanted me, and I needed Him.

Years have passed. God has made me strong, and the world has made me tough, but mostly I have learned how to rest in God's unceasing love and give it away.

I had to learn to be real. I had to own my sin and give it to the only One Who could make it disappear—Jesus, the real Prince Charming, Who provides us with an authentic happily-ever-after that lasts forever.

__Jan Brand__ is a freelance writer in Arlington, Texas. She is the former Assistant Director of North Texas Christian Writers, where she facilitated twenty-two writers' groups with a membership of more than three hundred writers. Her heart is to bring back the honor God once had in America. She currently serves as Vice President of Legislation for Republican Women of Arlington, where she advocates for religious freedom, and to restore truth in public education.

Thoughts to Ponder
from Finding the Real Prince Charming

1. We are not alone in the world.

2. Our lives have meaning.

3. We are loved by the God Who spoke the universe into being.

Knowing that Jesus paid for your sins, how excited are you to be loved?

When I am afraid,
I put my trust in you. — Psalm 56:3

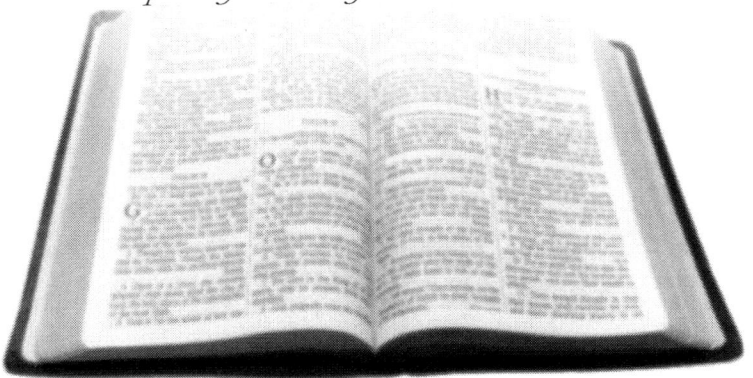

God Blessed Me with Childhood Cancer

by Brian McCollister

A cold sweat broke out on my brow as my heart beat violently. The lump forming inside my throat triggered a feeling of dread, deep dread.

Yes, there was no mistaking the sound of the ominous bone marrow procedure cart traveling toward my exam room. As the wheels click-clacked against the cold tile floor of the hallway, I heard the instruments jostling on the steel tray.

My first instinct was to run and hide. Running, however, was not an option, because a small group of nurses on standby were blocking the door. In my panic, I reasoned that if I crawled underneath the exam table, the doctor would never find me. *Yeah, that's the ticket.* I would become invisible, camouflaged among the table's wooden legs.

Of course, I was *very* visible.

As the door creaked open and the doctor's shadow darkened the entrance to the room, I contorted my body in a last-ditch effort to become one with the table.

The hair on my neck stood straight on end as I was pulled, screaming, from my make-shift hiding place and maneuvered onto the table, while the wax-like paper crinkled against my struggle. Resistance was futile. I was merely delaying the inevitable.

To neutralize me, a team of nurses wrestled me into something like a bear hug. I felt like I was suffocating underneath the weight.

Tears flowed uncontrollably down my cheeks.

I sensed the agony in my parents as my cries of resistance shattered their hearts.

"Mommy! Daddy! Why are you letting them do this to me?"

Gradually, a sense of impending doom grew inside my stomach. I knew precisely what was coming *next.*

An unmistakable odor of sterile alcohol filled my nostrils. I felt the damp swab run down my spine as the doctor prepped the target area. The pressure bearing down on me was almost unbearable, and my parched tongue panted for oxygen. My mind drifted to happier times as the 22-gauge needle plunged deep into my cartilage. Such was the life of a three-year-old with childhood cancer.

For most kids, nightmares involve monsters lurking underneath the bed. Mine were butterfly needles and spinal taps. But I did not *choose* these unpleasant dreams. *They* came to me.

"Though I walk in the midst of trouble, you preserve my life. . . . Your love, Lord, endures forever—do not abandon the works of your hands" (Psalm 138:7–8).

If I had to boil my entire life down into just two words, they would be "under construction." From my earliest memories until the present day, God has not been slack in keeping His promises to me. He is always working "under the hood" to perfect me. All the books in the world could not hold the countless wonders and works He has accomplished in my life. Some experiences were seared into my spirit through great pain, and those are the memories I can't forget.

For thirty-three months, I was a healthy little boy with no significant illnesses. On Saturday mornings, you would find me encamped by the family TV, enjoying my favorite cartoons while feasting on a warm bowl of Cream of Wheat.

I was increasingly aware of the baby girl growing inside Mom's tummy and was highly anticipating becoming a big brother in a few months.

In May 1984, a steady drip of mysterious ailments began to appear, and my pediatrician was on the case. A rogue lump over my eyebrow, which swelled when I was tired, was misdiagnosed as an eyebrow cyst.

As the months rolled on, the summer brought with it a revolving door of new symptoms: high fever, coughing, sore throat, pain in my arms, weakened leg strength, and more cysts. My doctor continued to observe me and run tests.

On September 20, God smiled on our family with the birth of my baby sister. The moment I saw her, I was captivated, determined to be the greatest big brother possible. For a time, everyone was happy to focus on some normalcy—until that fateful day in October when something went bump in twilight's wee hours of the night. I awoke to the realization that the paralyzing pain in my legs had returned.

As an abnormal amount of white blood cells rapidly accumulated in my body, my bone marrow expanded to accommodate the severe cellular overcrowding. My shins were daggers impaling the cluster of nerve endings in my legs, sending shockwaves of distress into my brainstem. In a desperate attempt to reach my parents, I climbed out of bed and collapsed on the floor with a thud.

One minute felt like an hour as the pulsating pain intensified in my legs. As I strained to move forward, I became aware of the warm glow of a lamp in the living room. Determined, I crawled toward the light.

It was 3:00 a.m., and Mom was awake, nursing my sister. With one look at me, she knew something was wrong. In addition to the searing pain in my legs, I was burning up.

The fever subsided by morning, and I went to preschool. When Mom arrived to pick me up, I was having difficulty walking again. My teacher advised us to get a second opinion and recommended another doctor.

Crisscross appointments and blood work with both doctors filled the afternoon. That evening, we were at my grandparents' house for dinner. As was the tradition, I made myself at home, playing on their floor, oblivious to the ashen complexion on my parents' faces.

They had just received a phone call with the test results. "I have bad news," the doctor said. "It's leukemia." He instructed them to take me immediately to St. Jude Children's Research Hospital in Memphis, where another doctor was waiting to take my case.

We had no idea that the next twenty-four hours would bring an extraordinary experience that would forever change us. God's plan for my life was about to commence.

By 8:30 p.m., we were headed to Tennessee on a relative's private plane. It was a "flight of faith." In the face of an unconquerable spirit of fear, faith was all my parents had to cling to. The possibility of losing their three-year-old son was unthinkable. So they had to place my young life in the Lord's hands.

18

At St. Jude, a representative in Admitting encouraged my parents to focus on getting me healthy rather than worry about the mounting expenses. Afterward, I had my initial examination. I was clueless as to what was happening. My parents assured me that these doctors would stop my legs from hurting.

About twelve hours after we received our second opinion, I was resting in a hospital room, hundreds of miles from home. Mom and Dad stayed in an adjoining family room, along with my grandmother and baby sister. But sleep would not visit my parents that night.

The next morning introduced us to my primary care doctor at St. Jude. My parents were impressed with his knowledge and were assured that they would take care of me. He wanted to run a battery of tests to pinpoint what type of leukemia I was fighting. I had no clue what that process entailed.

When my parents were told to stay in the waiting room, I broke out in a cold sweat. As strangers carried me away, I watched my mom and dad disappear behind the closing hallway doors.

I panicked.

That day marked my first spinal tap of many. It yielded the test results that my doctor needed. My pediatrician initially suspected we were dealing with AML (Acute Myeloid Leukemia) and estimated, if left untreated, I had only two weeks to live. My new doctor explained that we were dealing with ALL (Acute Lymphocytic Leukemia) instead. This type of cancer had a higher remission rate but was very aggressive. The treatment regimen must be equally offensive to hit the disease fast and hard. The road to remission would be long and harrowing, but for the first time, hope existed, despite the unknown.

Ask anyone who has experienced cancer, either through a loved one or personally, and they will testify to the brutality of chemotherapy. Drugs that the doctors pumped through my system were poisonous to my organs. But left untreated, I would have died from the cancer. They experimented with not just one but eight different drugs on me. The first two months of therapy proved exhausting. We spent two weeks in the hospital and six weeks at a local hotel. After a day of treatment, I would vomit off and on for about seven hours. Then, like clockwork, I felt better.

Due to the ravages of the powerful chemotherapy drugs on my body, routine blood draws at the lab were a dreadful experience. My veins radically shrank in size, and they had a penchant for running. I often joke that if I were a superhero, I would be The Veinless Wonder, mighty protector of the plasma, with powers to swiftly evade incoming harvesting attempts.

Webster's dictionary defines "needle" as "a slender hollow instrument for introducing material into or removing material from the body." The lab techs referred to them as "butterflies," which didn't make any sense, especially to a kid. Butterflies are beautiful insects, gracefully fluttering in the summer breeze. I wondered what depraved mind associated these majestic creations with a sharp tool that has more in common with a mosquito than a monarch butterfly.

As a frequent visitor, I became familiar with the skill level of each tech and how likely they were to "get it" on the first stick. Those elite few were some of my favorite ladies. But occasionally, if my veins were in an especially fickle mood, the tech embarked on a fishing expedition in search for a proper vein. To this day, I still get tingles just thinking about those sticks.

On my third day into treatment, I almost died after losing 50,000 white blood cells. As my kidneys worked overtime to flush out the dead cells, the blood drained from my head and left me as white as my bed sheets. My system was going into shock, because the body should not suddenly lose that many cells. The doctors placed me in Intensive Care to stabilize my blood pressure, which had plunged dangerously low. They reassured my parents that they could monitor my progress more closely this way.

Ten months into therapy, the Lord revealed to Mom that He had healed me. At the age of five-and-a-half, all chemotherapy ended. My doctors believed the cancer had left my body, but they still wanted me to return twice over the next year for additional testing. I remained in remission and returned to the hospital yearly for appointments until I turned eighteen. St. Jude officially discharges patients who have been off therapy over ten years from the ACT (After Completion of Therapy) clinic. They graduate and become St. Jude alumni.

During my three years of treatment, I underwent two-and-a-half years of chemotherapy and received countless bone marrow and spinal taps. Sixteen radiation treatments to the skull magically made my hair disappear. An endless marathon of blood tests and physical examinations confirmed my divine healing.

The apostle Paul writes about the ending of a significant chapter in life and the beginning of a new one. "When I was a child, I talked like a child, I thought like a child, I reasoned like a child. When I became a man, I put the ways of childhood behind me" (1 Corinthians 13:11). I reasoned that I was putting the diseases of childhood behind me and was pressing on toward my future. The Lord had healed me, and my session on the Potter's wheel was complete.

But God wasn't quite finished with me yet, as something ominous was growing inside me.

In the summer of 2003, I was getting ready to wrap up my senior year in college. On a last-chance vacation in Florida, I spent the day soaking up the sun with some friends, dreaming about post-graduate life. I slept hard that night—so hard that I was blissfully unaware of the bed violently shaking from my sudden convulsions.

When my consciousness returned, I found myself in the back of an ambulance with paramedics crowded around me. I had experienced a major grand mal seizure—symptom of a large meningioma that had been growing on my brain for over five years. The on-call doctor at the local emergency room delivered the news to my parents and mentioned that he wouldn't touch me "with a ten-foot pole."

Once again, we were without answers. Our hope, however, was in Jesus and the wonders He had performed for me in the past. So we prayed that the Lord would give us wisdom. Through several independent confirmations, God led us to a neurosurgeon in Shreveport, who was world-renowned for his work with brain tumors like mine. Once again, we had peace. He had extensive knowledge and had successfully operated on many. The benign tumor could still kill me, because it was dangerously compressing my brain. We later discovered that the meningioma was radiation-induced, directly connected to the treatments I had received as a kid.

With my faith firmly planted, we scheduled the craniotomy for August 25, 2003, my twenty-second birthday, of all days. This year would be the most memorable by far.

Growing up, I don't know if I ever fully appreciated the danger I was in from leukemia. But now, the stakes were much higher. After almost twenty years, I had so much more to lose— family, friends, life itself. Would God permit me to cheat death twice?

It was on the cold bathroom floor of a Memphis motel in 1985 that I had first learned to pray, begging God to remove my fear. The morning of the brain surgery, I was once again in a cold bathroom, pleading with the Lord for His peace. I could not "take this cup" of suffering without it. As I struggled to hear His voice, the lukewarm water flowed from the showerhead and mixed with the tears running down my face. The surgery prep team would arrive at any moment.

With a brave face, I hugged my family and loved ones extra tight. The team wheeled me down the hallway on the gurney, the wheels clicking across the tile floor. The realization dawned on me that the Lord was hiding His face, and I couldn't survive without Him. *Where are You, God? I need Your peace now.*

Right before the surgery team lifted me onto the procedure table, Jesus revealed Himself to me in an unprecedented way. The moment that my back contacted the chilled steel, warmth washed over me, bathing me in a peace that made no scientific sense. He was God of the *last second*. Fresh tears of joy streamed from my eyes as I felt the Lord's tight embrace. While the anesthesia lulled me to sleep, fear instantly fled from my spirit.

Several hours later, I was in recovery. Just like a dormant supercomputer, my mind was a blank screen with a small blinking dot. My consciousness returned with a surge as the power was suddenly restored. My brain was rebooting. Following a five-year oppression by the meningioma, the affected areas of my frontal lobes were increasingly aware of their newfound emancipation—and those synapses were ready to fire once again.

My hearing returned first. Strange noises became louder, as if someone were rotating the volume knob. Confusion set in, as my vision was still offline. In the darkness, I struggled to pinpoint the sources of the sounds. In my mind's eye, I imagined a performance theater with the curtains closed. Suddenly, they began to rise as I heard an audible countdown from ten to one. *Snap!* My blindness was gone, and the distinct sensation of tears overflowed as a silent cry of praise swelled up from inside my being. Deep bellows of heaving sobs escaped my chest as the sensation in my hands and feet returned.

Joy overflowed from my heart with the realization that I wasn't paralyzed—the greatest birthday gift ever. Looking back, I think I may have resembled Dick Van Dyke, pointing my fingers and clicking my heels together as if I were performing a horizontal tap dance.

My family arrived and celebrated with me, along with our neurosurgeon, who confidentially reported that the surgery was successful. The unwelcome intruder had been evicted from my skull. He said that if the tumor had not been attached to the meninges tissue, it would have jumped out.

A potent cocktail of anesthesia and pain killers ensured that I would drift in and out of consciousness for the remainder of the afternoon. The ICU was a gloomy place of isolation and helplessness, even during the daytime. But as the sun set and visiting hours wound down, panic gripped me when I said goodnight and I watched my family walk away.

The lights faded, and the strange noises returned. Darkness weighed down upon me, and the shadows came alive. As my brain reeled from the trauma, my skull strained to accommodate the swelling. My mind was in overdrive and began to play tricks on me, beginning a slow descent into madness.

Blood-curdling screams came from the partition on either side of my bed. People I hadn't seen in years were gathered in the room, staring at me with evil intentions.

I recognized a doctor passing by, and I tried to alert him to the struggle happening next door. He turned to enter the curtain, pausing to glance in my direction. I watched in sheer terror as his eyes glowed a bright demonic red. I was hallucinating heavily, trapped inside a morphine-induced haze. There were no familiar faces of family or friends to be found. I felt hopelessly alone, forsaken by God in my personal Sheol.

My only companion that night was a strange lady who sat staring at me from a lone chair at the end of my bed. I didn't know she was the night nurse assigned to me. The last thing I remember was her walking toward my IV pump, and then, mercifully, everything went black.

Early the next day, God "lifted me from the miry clay" when my neurosurgeon arranged for me to be transported to a regular room ahead of schedule. The reports he received on my fragile mental state were highly concerning.

My recovery progressed rapidly. Within a week, I was discharged, and I headed to college for my last semester. But within only a few days of being back in class, I had to withdraw because of an infection in the wound.

I woke up one morning in a pool of spinal fluid on my pillow. Another surgery was immediately scheduled. Though I could not make sense of this unforeseen inconvenience, the doctors discovered that this infection was successful in eating away some remaining tumor cells that had survived the first craniotomy. This was just another instance of the Lord continuing to "perfect" me. What a good, good Father.

Over the last decade, I've had the chance to pay forward and participate in several long-term follow-up studies through St. Jude. These "life studies" measure residual side effects from the treatments, including sleep habits, bone flexibility, reflex response, pulmonary function, and memory retention.

There's also a psychological component to the studies, where social workers investigate the survivor's emotional health and mental stability. These are the sessions I look forward to the most, because it's just another opportunity to share my story.

People ask, "Looking back, do you have bitterness about the disease? Do you ever wonder, *Why me?* when you look at everything you had to go through?"

I think they are usually taken aback by my response.

"Actually," I say, "if I had the chance, I would do it all again." *Whoa.* How can I say that? Would I genuinely want to endure all the pain, all the hardships, the emotional devastation, and personal setbacks? In a word, "Yes."

I'm alive, and I have a stronger faith in the God of the

impossible. Although I accepted the Lord when I was six years old, He has used my entire life to bring me closer to Him and cause me to recognize my full dependence on Him and His grace. I am a mess—a wretch—needing His love and forgiveness every day, so I try to be mindful of that truth as I strive to hear His voice.

These tragic experiences served to mold me into the person I am today and gave me an up-close and personal encounter with the Lord's mercy and goodness. Having faced death so early, I have a deeper spiritual maturity than most people have. And though I paid a heavy price for this pearl, I can see the leukemia and subsequent brain tumors for what they are—gifts from God. I often wonder where, or *who,* I would be without them. The scars on my body are souvenirs from the miracles that the Lord performed.

If you are facing an impossible situation, and you feel alone in your battle, there is good news. The Lord has not forsaken you. The Bible says that God brings happiness from sadness: "You turned my wailing into dancing; you removed my sackcloth and clothed me with joy" (Psalm 30:11). Only Jesus can take catastrophic events and turn them into fond memories and opportunities to glorify Him for everyone who hears your story.

I've also accepted the fact that there's no estimated date of completion for my life. True "perfection" will only happen when I finally behold His beautiful face in eternity—and that's enough for me.

Bless His holy name.

Brian McCollister is a wretch without the Almighty's daily love and grace. Through the many trials in his life, he has become acquainted with the suffering of many and has a love for encouraging people and praying for the sick. He serves on the hospital visitation team at Healing Place, his home church. As a media producer, Brian has a passion for helping others share their testimonies through personal documentaries. He enjoys blogging and public speaking. Brian resides in Baton Rouge, Louisiana, with his wife of ten years, Chipley. In May of 2017, they became the proud parents of boy and girl twins. He can be reached at Brian@Persongraphy.com.

Thoughts to Ponder
from God Blessed Me with Childhood Cancer

1. God's peace is always on time.

2. Never take your health for granted.

3. Always keep a heavenly perspective.

**What are some ways
God is "perfecting" your life?**

*We know that in all things God works for the good
of those who love Him, who have been called
according to his purpose. — Romans 8:28*

Not a Normal Day
by Donna Renay Patrick

When a new year dawns, many people make New Year's resolutions for new beginnings, new goals, and turnarounds. I have not made a New Year's resolution since January 27, 1983. That was the day my family's life changed—forever.

The year 1983 was supposed to be "my year." I had set all sorts of goals. I had a dream. It was the year to make things happen. My job for the past two years was one that I obtained right out of college. I had no plans to stay there forever, but it was a pretty good start. My plan was to go to law school, and this job was preparing me for that. Later, I learned that it would have no bearing at all on my performance in law school. However, it would have a bearing on future employment opportunities.

After graduating from college, I went to work for the Dallas County District Clerk's office. It was just a clerical position, but the salary was decent—enough to pay the rent and put some money away. While I had worked during the summers in high school, this was my first taste of the "real world" in terms of gainful employment. I did not have Mom and Dad to fall back on. This was my job, my money, my rent, my budget, and my responsibility. I also had a second job as a church musician, which meant rehearsals at least twice a week, two services on Sunday, and an occasional wedding or funeral. I was living on my own, and life was good.

My mother was overprotective. When I informed her that I wasn't coming back home to Illinois following my graduation from Bishop College in Dallas, Texas, her remedy was to move to Dallas to be close to her two children—me and my sister. My sister, Jackye, had begun a life here in Dallas when she graduated a few years earlier. My mom did not tell a living soul she was moving here. She just did it. She showed up at my church one Sunday morning with no warning.

My first thoughts were not happy thoughts. My sister and I worried that she had come only to spy on us. However, we later understood that she just wanted to be closer to her children.

Little did anyone know that the bottom would soon fall out of our lives.

It was a normal Thursday, or so I thought. I was at work, helping criminal defense lawyers file their motions. I struggled to read the judge's handwritten instructions on each case's docket sheet so I could submit paperwork to the sheriff's office, dictating, per the judge's order, whether or not a prisoner was to be released from the county jail or remain there.

During the afternoon, I was unaware that Jackye was fighting for her life. She was living in the Oak Cliff section of Dallas. She had taught high school biology for several years and coached the girls' volleyball, basketball, and track teams. She consistently produced state champions. She eventually left her teaching job to embark on entrepreneurship. I was at work with no clue that a man, with nothing else to do, picked that day to burglarize my mother's home, where both my mother and sister lived. Jackye's car had broken down earlier that day, and she had it towed to the auto shop for repair. Not seeing her car outside, the intruder assumed no one was home, but he carried a weapon on his unsolicited visit anyway.

When I learned that all this happened while I was at work, I felt guilty. My sister was in grave danger, and I was not there to help. My normal Thursday routine was to come home from work, change clothes, and head to choir rehearsal. On this particular day, my phone rang as I was getting dressed. Rehearsal was at 7:00 p.m., so this call had to have come between 6:00 and 6:30. It was my pastor. We had a great working relationship, but it was unusual for him to call me at home. I did not detect any concern in his voice until he asked me if I was on my way to my mother's house. When I said no, there was deafening silence on the other end of the phone. Then he said, "You don't know about Jackye?" I knew something was awry, so without answering his question, I told him I would call my mother's house and call him right back.

When I called Mother's house, a friend of my sister's answered. He told me that someone had hurt Jackye. He did his best to use kind words that would tell me she was dead. He had found her lying in a pool of blood on the kitchen floor, near the back door. She had called him, as well as the police, when she knew someone was trying to break into the house. I learned the details in the days that followed, but I knew enough at that point to realize I had to come up with a way to tell my mother that her oldest child had been brutally killed. I didn't know how I was going to do that.

Keeping my word to my pastor, I called him back in tears. I told him I would see him shortly. I called my Minister of Music, telling him I wouldn't be at rehearsal. Right before I left my apartment, my phone rang. It was one of the musicians at the church. She had learned what had happened and begged me not to drive myself. She wanted to pick me up. I didn't accept her kind invitation. What I did do was agree to stop at her house, since it was on the way.

When I got to my friend's house, she drove me to my mother's home. Many people were gathered in the living room, including my pastor. There were some people present who didn't even like me, so I wondered why they were there. It certainly wasn't because they cared about me.

Among the people in the house were two Dallas police officers. What was even more heartbreaking than the fact that Jackye was now lying in the county morgue, was that no one responded when she called 9-1-1. Thirty-three minutes went by before help actually arrived. When her friend arrived and found her, he called 9-1-1, and it was *his* call they responded to, not hers. Had she gotten medical attention sooner, she might have lived. We'll never know.

My mother wasn't home from work yet, so she had no idea what had happened. The police officers wanted to get her and bring her home, but I asked them not to. This was their normal practice in situations like this. I asked them to let her come home, because as soon as they showed up at her job, she would know something was wrong. With some coaxing, they agreed.

When Mom got there, she immediately knew something was terribly wrong. The house was full of people, cars were outside, and she didn't see Jackye. She panicked when she saw me crying. Jackye didn't answer when she called her name. I still didn't know how to tell her she had to make preparations to bury her oldest child, but I thank God for my pastor, who took my mother into another room to explain what had happened. I will always be grateful to him for that.

As the details continued to unfold, my father, another trusted family friend, and other relatives arrived in town. We learned that the man who committed this heinous act lived in the neighborhood. His grandfather lived across the street and came over to tell us he had heard his grandson talking about breaking into somebody's house. He was convinced that his grandson had done it. This news upset Mom terribly, but that wasn't his intent. He only wanted Mom to know. And then he left.

We had been planning a surprise birthday party for Jackye on the following Saturday. Her birthday was January 29th. Instead of a birthday party, we were planning her funeral. She had been stabbed nine times and was left to drown in her own blood. As the police and the district attorney's office investigated, it was concluded from the six wounds in her back that Jackye had been trying to get away. There were also "defense wounds" on her hands, which meant she put up a good fight. Unfortunately, she was no match for the killer's butcher knife.

My mother stopped living after that. Oh, she was alive, but very near to a walking dead person. This was the first time death had come to our immediate family, so it was an exceptionally difficult time. Parents never expect to bury one of their children. Jackye had always been there. Now she wasn't. My mom had friends over the years who had buried a child, but never in her wildest dreams did she think she would experience something like that.

I have always been the strong type, and as painful as it was, I tried to be strong for my mom. That was a mistake, not for my mom, but for me.

A few days after the funeral, we tried to get back to life as our new normal, but in keeping my pain inside and trying to be strong for Mom, I fell into terrible depression. I went to work, to church, to my rehearsals, and *functioned*, but I kept to myself. I handled my responsibilities, but I couldn't wait to go home and just cry.

I cried all the time.

Perhaps it was delayed grief. I was so busy holding up for Mom that I didn't do my own grieving. Not being able to pray was the worst part. I wasn't angry with God, but I didn't know what to say in prayer. I went to church, but I was very detached emotionally and spiritually. I went to choir rehearsals, unprepared to teach or play anything. Then I had the nerve to get mad at my Minister of Music when he talked to me about my newfound irresponsibility.

At work, I was really a mess. I was cross with everybody, terribly unfocused, and I wasn't performing up to standard. Knowing that the person who killed my sister was awaiting trial in the county jail, two floors above me, didn't help. I shut out my friends. While I never considered suicide, I was okay with the thought of having a really bad car accident. That way, I would be injured severely enough that I would just sleep. When I was asleep, I wouldn't think about how deeply I was hurting inside. My mom knew what bad shape I was in, emotionally, and she tried to help. But it just wasn't possible.

Even though I shut most everybody out, I was blessed with caring friends and co-workers who checked on me anyway. They were concerned. They tried to understand what I was going through, but again, I wasn't open to their attempts to help me. I wanted no one. I was in my own grief-stricken world. I didn't want the pain, yet I was somehow comfortable with it.

The depression went on for several months. Prayer had always been a part of my Christian experience. But in the emotional state I was in, all I could say to the Lord before bed was, "Thank You, Lord, for bringing me through another day." And in the morning I would say, "Thank You, Lord, for giving me another day." That was the extent of my prayers.

The turnaround came when I had reached a place of total surrender. I let go of the grief so I could begin to heal. When I truly gave my grief to God, He gave me a new mindset. I began to experience the healing I desperately needed. When I was able to pray again, I surrendered all my pain to Him. Then my life changed. I still had to adjust to a new normal—living without the best big sister ever. I also learned how God will carry you when you cannot carry yourself. He is a friend like no other when we are hurting. He proved how much He loved me, and how He held me close to Him. I just didn't realize it, because I was in a cage of depression.

There was a jury trial, and my sister's killer received a sixty-year prison sentence. Justice didn't bring Jackye back. We still had to make the transition of learning to live without her, but God is faithful. After about five years, my mother began to live again.

I am a survivor. I am a fighter. But I didn't survive in my own strength—it was all God. My sister was a beautiful young woman with an upbeat personality, pretty brown eyes, an infectious laugh, a melodious singing voice, and lots of ambition. She saw a bright future for herself. God had other plans, but I am so grateful for the time we had to be a family. I will always cherish that.

Donna Renay Patrick is an award-winning author of two praise and worship-themed devotionals: At All Times *and* It's In Your Praise. *She also co-authored two other devotionals, one to encourage women in the workplace called,* Be Refreshed, *and the other a stewardship-themed devotional entitled,* The Perfect Seven. *She is a musician, worship leader, transformational speaker, and host of The Donna Patrick Show, an internet-based segment that emphasizes the priority of worship in the 21st century church, and next-level personal and corporate worship. She writes and speaks often on how your worship, purpose, and leadership are interrelated. Visit her website at* **DonnaRenayPatrick.com.**

Thoughts to Ponder

from Not a Normal Day

1. When you need help, ask God.

2. Allow other caring people to help during your grief process.

3. When experiencing grief, take time off as needed.

> **How do you trust God rather than handle loss in your own strength?**

Therefore we do not lose heart. Though outwardly we are wasting away, yet inwardly we are being renewed day by day. — 2 Corinthians 4:16

Daughter of the King
by Anna Marie Valden

The large yellow school bus stopped in front of my house, where a group of us kids played, including me, my two younger brothers, and a gaggle of neighborhood friends. The bus belonged to a local church that I was familiar with because of its size.

I grew up Baptist, as my grandfather was a self-ordained minister who preached at tent revivals. However, unlike the tent revivals, the folks on the bus threw out candy to entice us to listen and go on an outing the next day. They said, "Be back at eight in the morning with your parents' permission" (like mine would be up that early on a Sunday). I doubted my mom and dad would miss us, probably not until the street lights came on that night. I argued with my brothers. I told them the church was using a lot of cheap tricks, and it was not a church we needed to go to. The candy won.

The next morning, the bus took us to a remote property with a huge house, barns, and even a pond. It was the pastor's house. I had never seen so much opulence in my life. As we toured the property, I saw carpeted walls in the garage—for noise control. Heavy red draperies hung around the master bed, also for noise control, with a crown suspended from the ceiling over the bed, with a mirror. I was disgusted by the display.

When we got home, I was determined to find a good church.

The next Sunday, I walked to the end of our block, where I heard cheering and laughter. I crossed the wooded space to discover a baseball game being played in a field behind a small white church with a steeple. I watched the game until someone shouted, "You wanna play?" I ran as fast as I could to join the game.

I loved this church, and the people quickly became my pseudo-family, because chaos filled my own family life. With an alcoholic stepfather and a prescription-addicted mother, I always had to be on guard. At church, I sang in the choir, played with the babies in the nursery, and joined in praise and worship.

Then came the day of the altar call. I was spiritually led and compelled to surrender my heart and life to Jesus in an easy and simple prayer. I returned home that Sunday to tell my mom the glorious news. I was saved and ready to be baptized. Unfortunately, she became angry and said I had no idea what I was doing. There was no way I would be allowed back at that church, let alone be baptized at the age of eight.

We moved shortly after that, and my mother then allowed my biological father back into my life. All his parental rights had been stripped away during their divorce, and when he re-entered my life, he turned out to be anything but a "father" figure. From age nine to seventeen, I was abused in every conceivable way. I learned to keep secrets, to do as I was told, and to put on a happy face.

I married at the age of nineteen. I thought it was love. I married a man I thought would love me, who would never cheat, lie, abandon, or abuse me like my father had. I was wrong. Little girls often grow up to marry their father-figures. Like my father, he never left a mark that anyone could see. The problem was that slowly, after isolating me from family, friends, and church, I began to believe his lies.

What lies have you accepted in your life?

To get along, I had to play nice, dress the way I was expected to, keep an immaculate house, go to dinner at the clubs, and attend church—smiling to show that everything was grand, when all I felt like was a fraud. Nothing was ever good enough or like it should be. I became someone I didn't know, and I prayed for change.

After thirty-one years of marriage, I divorced and took off my ring. I was yanked from my prisoner-of-privilege life to being a fifty-plus single mom with an adult daughter, Dawn, who had IDD—Intellectual and Developmental Delays. I always knew she was my responsibility and would be with me for the remainder of my life. My three other daughters were supportive, but they had their own lives and daughters to care for.

At the time of the divorce, my youngest daughter was seventeen, although developmentally she would always be ten. I lived with "Peter Pan." Working a full eight-hour day would be difficult, because I was limited to how long I could leave her alone. Left to her own devices, she might walk out of the apartment, eat whatever she liked, and not do any of the self-care things she should, like brushing her teeth. I took low-paying writing jobs so I could be available to her. That work wasn't enough to support us, so I tried to get her into support services. However, since we had moved from one county to another, I had to reapply for everything. The county we were in simply said, "No, we have no services to offer her at this time."

I couldn't get services, because my alimony/child support was too high, although her father hadn't paid anything after finding out his girlfriend was pregnant. I had been a career mom. I could stretch a pound of hamburger four days—but how does that translate to life-sustaining job skills? It doesn't. Because I had no job history, my unemployment paid a meager $62 a month.

Dawn couldn't get Social Security, because they considered the income she should have from child support. I couldn't qualify for food stamps, because they considered the child support as part of my income, even though I wasn't getting any. I lost my car. I sold everything else of value. My dog died the day I was released from the hospital for the third time with ketoacidosis, a potentially deadly result of not having the right insulin as a Type 1 diabetic. We were dead in the water. I sold my pearls, class ring, and wedding ring to make rent, and I collected food from the food bank.

When attending Gateway Church, someone told me about their care program. I reached out to them and to the Jewish Family Services center. With their help, I was able to keep my apartment one more month. In late November, I got a call from Alexander Milne. When you have a child/adult with IDD, the one thing you do upon diagnosis is apply for everything, including future facility living, because one day you will die, and you must make accommodations for your child. If you don't, who knows what can happen? Alexander Milne was one of those lists that Dawn had been on for at least two years. They called to say, "We have a house for her."

Dawn was so excited. She had been saying she wanted to leave home and go out on her own like her sisters. I went through the motions, thinking, *Okay, this is best*. Deep in my heart, I felt more and more like a failure as a mom—like Abraham being told to sacrifice his child to prove his heart was trusting of God. But like Gideon, every step of the way I prayed for confirmation. I was always met with peace about the facility, the people, and the process.

On February 14, 2017, what would have been my thirty-fifth wedding anniversary, her father and I drove Dawn nine hours to her new home. After two days of settling her in, I left. A friend who understood my situation drove me home. I walked into my empty apartment and shattered into a million lonely pieces. I felt like the worst mother in the world. Because I was unable to care for my daughter, I had to send her away. I took off my apron because I felt I no longer deserved the title of mother.

What kind of mother does that? I was angry with God. I felt like He allowed the decades of abuse from my father, my husband, and now He had taken away the one thing I cared about most: my daughter. I didn't want to face the fact that many of my choices had consequences. Left alone now, I could reflect on the choices I had made—the denial, the abortion, the infidelities, and the lies—all of it. I had to admit that I had some responsibility in why I was where I was. The abuse was the evil act of another person, and I had to give that to God.

One morning, I screamed at God, "Are You trying to kill me?" A tender answer resonated in my heart. *Yes.* He had been working to kill the other me so He could bring the true me back to Him, to bring me back to that little girl, the one in the chapel on bended knee, asking for salvation. With my hair finally loose and free the way I wanted to wear it, I was shown how I could let go and trust Him.

What do you blame God for?

I learned that God was there all along, keeping my precious little eight-year-old's soul in His hands, safe and sound. What others did to me damaged only my flesh, not my soul. I began looking at my blessings outside my own needs. My daughter was safe, happy, and well cared for. A willingness to serve and not be served became overwhelming. As I grew in my journey, I trusted that I was saved. I am Anna Marie, mother, grandmother, sister, aunt, and beloved daughter of the King of kings. I reestablished my commitment with a simple prayer:

Jesus, I recognize that I am a sinner and need You. I believe You are the Son of God, that You died on the cross for my sins, and then rose from the dead to sit at the right hand of God. I receive You as my Lord and Savior. I surrender my will to You, and I choose to follow You. Amen.

Anna Marie Valden is a published author and award-winning poet. She is also a publisher with Dragonfly Press and Lord Strong Publishing. She lives in Dallas, Texas, with her Chihuahua, Chloe.

Thoughts to Ponder
from Daughter of the King

1. We are sons and daughters of the King of kings.

2. We can be healed emotionally from the most horrific of violations.

3. God wants to provide the best answer for our needs.

When have you blamed God for the trials in your life?

And my God will meet all your needs according to the riches of his glory in Christ Jesus. — Philippians 4:19

Loss of a Child
by Mitch Land

My wife, Lea, wanted to go to Toronto from Dallas by car—via
Maine. I wasn't interested in going anywhere. I was content
working at the University of North Texas, where I was teaching
and directing the journalism graduate program. In fact, the first
day of our vacation, we took all day to pack the car to set out in
the afternoon, but we couldn't agree on where to go or when to
go. I was frustrated. I really wanted to unpack and just stay in
the house. But Lea was determined to go to Maine and Toronto.

She saw my eyebrows wince and knew I was disturbed. As we
studied the map, we realized it would take twelve hours to go to
Toronto from Maine.

Lea smiled. "Let's just go to a movie this afternoon. We don't
have to go now." She chuckled, and I broke into a half smile.
"Let's go tomorrow morning early," she said, "straight to
Canada."

This decision lifted the burden from my mind, and I
immediately felt relieved.

We called our surprised daughter, Mae Beth, to inform her
that we hadn't departed yet and decided to go to a movie, *The
Mummy*, starring Brandon Frasier.

Early Thursday morning, June 10, 1999, we started our trip to
Ontario by way of upstate New York and Niagara Falls.

Although our two weeks in New York and Algonquin
Provincial Park in Ontario were special and gave us an
opportunity to enjoy each other and wind down from a busy
year, there wasn't anything particularly spiritual for me. We
observed the Lord's Supper every evening, and Lea prayed for
me, as she had done almost every night since January 1998. I
now realize that my precious wife was doing spiritual warfare
over me during those many months.

For three years, Lea had only part of me, because I was still
mourning for our son, Austin. After he was killed at the age of
twenty-two by a drunk driver, I hadn't been able to shake the
sorrow that continually gnawed on my bones. Even as we
worshipped in church, I couldn't enter praise without thinking

how much our son loved God, had been faithful, and had danced with great joy in the Lord before the altar of our church, Shady Grove, in Grand Prairie.

I wouldn't allow myself to be happy. Each time I thought about my life without Austin, my heart broke all over again. When I spoke to crowds about the horror of losing a loved one to drunk-driving crashes, I relived the nightmare and could scarcely speak without crying.

Lea told me that bitterness lay behind those tears as I spoke to the crowds. People may not have sensed it. They were always so kind, understanding, and loving. But Lea knew me. My spiritual man was lost—to both my wife and God.

Oh, I would pray. I said, "God didn't take my son. Sin did." I mustered enough courage to say, "I still have four children, although one has been killed. I know where he is—dancing on golden streets."

Austin's favorite praise song was "We Will Dance." Part of the chorus said we would dance on golden streets with our glorious King. We had the engraver put HE IS DANCING ON STREETS THAT ARE GOLDEN on his tombstone. My mind said many of these things to people, but my heart couldn't receive them.

Alone with God, I cried, "Oh God, where is my little boy? I couldn't protect him. I couldn't keep him from being hurt. Where were you God? Why didn't you send those angels my wife always talks about? Where were Austin's angels? Had they taken a coffee break?"

I never said aloud that I blamed God for Austin's death, but inwardly I did.

Grief is a normal process that we must pass through, but I let it give the enemy a foothold in my heart and life. My flesh suppressed my spiritual man. I didn't enjoy going to church, praising God, reading the Bible, or even praying with Lea. I just went through the motions like so many other meaningless rituals.

I resented having the Lord's Supper with Lea every evening. I submitted to it because I knew she was right. It was my Christian duty to observe the Lord's suffering for our sins.

I took comfort from Lea's praying over me. She rubbed my

shoulders and back and just loved me through the valley of this shadow of death. Still, my flesh was fully in control.

Sometimes I cried to God, "Oh, Father, is any of this real? Oh, please! Let it be real. Please just be there with Austin. Why do You make it so hard to hear and see You?"

One day, I fell on the floor and screamed, "God, why don't You stop this madness?" I thought about the millions of Jews who died in the Holocaust. I thought about the 500,000 who were butchered in Rwanda. "Why, God? What are You waiting for? Where are You?" Blaming God, I felt deep resentment, even though I quickly added, "I'm sorry, God. I know I must live by faith through this."

I remembered how Austin and our third son, Andrew, had experienced a renewal in the Holy Spirit. Austin knew about the Spirit-filled life. He had even accompanied Dion Robert's group to Bouake, Ivory Coast, and was touched by the Spirit when he was a little boy.

In October 1995, Austin, Andrew, and Andrew's fiancée, Megan, went to see firsthand what people were calling "The Toronto Blessing." People were being filled with the Holy Spirit, falling out in the Spirit, manifesting in curious ways. By then, thousands of people were flocking to Toronto to learn about the move of God. The international press—including Peter Jennings of ABC News—was broadcasting stories about the phenomena.

When they returned, we could tell their lives had been radically transformed by the Holy Spirit. Megan began shaking under the power of the Holy Spirit. Knowing Megan's humility, I knew she would never do this in her flesh.

Austin was so filled by the power of God that when he prayed for people—even those who were standing across a room with their backs turned—they would fall to the ground. When I looked deep into his eyes, icy chills consumed me, because I saw that God had changed him.

We rejoiced in what the Spirit was doing in the lives of our two sons. Austin begged us to go with him and Andrew to Eaglemount Church in Lewisville, to the Friday night renewal meetings. I didn't want to wait long into the night for people to pray for me. I had already been filled with the Spirit. I didn't

42

need to stand at the front for twenty minutes while people prayed over me. I didn't want to stand there, waiting to be "slain in the Spirit." I didn't mind if others did that, but I didn't want to.

I watched in delight as my sons danced, sang, and shouted the praises of God. I was content that my *children* were moving with God. They didn't just move. They *ran* with God. All they wanted to do was praise and pray and soak in the Lord.

My life was fulfilled in my children—my sons, my daughter, and my beautiful wife. They were my trophies, my miracles of God. We were happy just worshipping God as a family at Shady Grove. I was content to have beautiful children who loved the Lord. My heart swelled with joy when people commented on how handsome and wonderful our sons and daughter were. Many were impressed by the intensity of worship our children displayed.

Then, our world was shattered. Just as we were experiencing a wondrous, magical time together, sin ripped out a quarter of our heart. A man and his friends exited Café 121 in Lewisville on February 21 around 11:30 p.m.—about as drunk as anyone can be. His friends wanted to drive him home. Instead, he took off in his big blue truck, heading north in the southbound lane of Highway 121.

At the same time, Austin had just left his fiancée, Ashli, at her home after a date. In his Honda Civic, he was on his way to work at Federal Express, driving south. He and Ashli had argued over something. After he left, Ashli felt disappointment that they had words over something silly.

To find comfort, Austin engaged the tape player with Brian Doerksen's "Eternity." I imagine that the Holy Spirit comforted his heart as he listened to the promises of eternity. I can imagine a smile on his face as all fear of the future disappeared with the words "no more fear" intoned. Because we retrieved the tape lodged in the player, we know he was listening to this song when the monster truck slammed head-on into the Honda.

The truck was traveling at 70 mph. The impact crushed Austin's chest despite the air bag. A policeman said Austin was alive when he got to the scene. He never told me if Austin was conscious. I want to believe that he felt no pain.

For weeks after Austin's death, the image of his broken, bleeding body trapped behind the wheel haunted me. I thought, *I couldn't take care of him. I couldn't be there to hold him, to bring comfort to him.* It brought back the painful memory of his birth, when we thought he would die of hyaline membrane disease. As I observed my newborn son lying emaciated in an incubator, I felt so helpless. I revisited images of me as a young father standing behind the glass window of the hospital nursery as tears poured down my face. My mother reassured me, saying, "Austin isn't dead, Mitchell. He's alive! Get hold of yourself."

Lea had such faith that God would heal him. As she lay there in pain from the Caesarian section, she smiled and said, "He'll be all right. God will heal him."

Her mother and I knelt at Lea's bedside and prayed for Austin's healing.

A few hours later, the physician said Austin was getting better. "I don't know what happened," he said, "but during the night, he began recovering."

I said, "I know God has used you to bring healing to him."

"Oh no," he said. "I didn't do anything. It had to be God."

My little son was healed, and we often celebrated.

And now, my twenty-two-year-old boy lay dead. My dreams for him were shattered. The hopes of conducting his wedding, of holding his children, of watching him mature as a husband and father—all were lost.

It didn't matter that nine people, most of whom didn't even know one another, told us of visions they had of Austin in Heaven. My heart didn't change as Barbara Rabon announced that she had seen Austin standing arm-in-arm beside the Savior, both grinning from ear to ear. When she gave us the prints she had commissioned a Christian artist to draw, my heart was blessed but not healed.

One Sunday morning, the sorrow that engulfed my face caused Monte Smith to stop leading the worship service. He asked the congregation to pray just for me. Still no healing. For three years, my heart broke, time after time.

Lea kept saying, "Mitchell, Austin is in Heaven. We'll be there with him someday."

I said, "I hope you're right."

44

Lea often prayed, "God, just post angels around the children."

I wanted to challenge her every time. *Well, where were* Austin's *angels?* At least twice, I said that to her. Only my desire to withhold my bitterness kept me from saying it more often.

The Toronto meeting we attended was titled, Festival of Joy, the same type of conference my children had attended. I hadn't known joy in so long. I knew too that I had been walking in the flesh for three years. I had become "soulish," as deceased ministry leader, John Paul Jackson, often said. My joy had always been centered in my children—even more than in my wife. My children had become my idols.

Often, I tell fathers, "Nothing you will ever do will top these children God has given you."

My heart still rejoices as I think of my children and grandchildren. But when Austin was killed, this joy was wounded. The center of my life was ripped apart. I willed my spirit to plunge into a well of sadness while I attempted to soothe my body and soul with the things of this world.

We arrived two days early for the conference—June 21, 1999. I was a bit miffed at Lea for not having verified the date. After all, I thought we could have taken in more of the sights north of Ontario, where it wasn't so hot.

But in her usual way, Lea knew what to say to cheer me up. "We can go to a movie! We'll just make the most of it." She must have thought, *If I can't see him happy in the Lord, I can figure out how to make him content in the world.* We went to see *The General's Daughter.* Like so many times before, I lost my thoughts in the beautiful cinematography, which I considered a work of art. But my heart did not need the troubling subject matter.

The next evening, it was easy to agree to go to the service with Lea. I thought, *After all, we did go to a movie last night. This is the least I can do.* We enjoyed the worship service and the peaceful atmosphere of the church. As I gazed at the front row where I had seen on a videotape Austin standing with uplifted arms worshipping God, the anguish of my loss gripped me. I wept as I thought about where he might have stood, how he loved God. I wondered, *Did they stand there? Am I sitting in the chair Austin sat in?* Tears streamed down my face. I cried inside, *Oh God, why?*

Where is my baby? I longed to run home and hide from this grief.

The next morning, Festival of Joy began with intercessory prayer and praise. We were blessed, but nothing changed in my heart.

I enjoyed the preaching of Joseph Garlington. His blending of preaching and singing delighted my heart. But when Joseph said, "Turn to your neighbor and say . . ." the same critical attitude spurt from my heart like venom, because I resented this "manipulation." I thought, *Why do these preachers continually have us repeat words as if we're third graders?* I resolved not to respond at all to their constant badgering. Even as Jeremy Sinnott followed Garlington's penchant for collective mimicry, I resisted. "I don't like being a puppet on a string," I said to Lea, grumbling. Oh yes, the soulish man still ruled.

Lea rebuked me. "Mitchell, watch your attitude."

After three days, I became restless. I said to Lea, "Well, just two more days, and we go home."

Her smile relaxed. "You want to go home now, don't you?" She longed for God to touch me.

During the time of intercessory prayer, she pleaded with God to reach into my hardened heart. "Oh God," she prayed, "I just don't have the strength to go on this way. I'm ready to give up. I'm so tired of leading this ghost of a man."

She had grown weary of the burden of a wounded and weak husband who refused to be her spiritual leader. She came to what she considered the last resort, the last stop. She could no longer hold this broken father. She could no longer be his spiritual Florence Nightingale. She decided to go with God, with or without me.

As the conference ended on Saturday night, I asked Lea, "Do you still want to stay through Sunday night?" I hoped she would agree to leave Sunday after the morning worship service. I would have been delighted to leave Toronto on Saturday.

"Oh yes, Mitchell," she said firmly. "We have to stay." Her response nailed the decision. I knew better than to argue.

Paul Oakley was scheduled to speak, but apparently had returned to England with David Fellingham, because Jeremy Sinnott took the pulpit. My critical spirit surged as Jeremy droned on and on, repeating himself, preaching truisms I had heard a hundred times before. As his wife, Connie, took the mic, I thought, *Oh no. Now she'll repeat everything Jeremy just said.*

I wanted the meeting to end. I was tired. I wanted to go home. I wanted to return to the comfort of my office at the university, where I could forget my sorrow. I wanted to cover myself in my professional concerns, my new position, my pride, my children, myself, my needs, my entertainment.

Jeremy interrupted my rebellious thoughts with a challenge to search our life memories for those we had not forgiven. I thought about the high school boys who used to make fun of me. Reluctantly, I obeyed and inserted their names in the phrase, "God, I forgive _____ for _____," joining the chorus of prayers rising from the congregation.

But Jeremy insisted again, saying, "Now, make sure you haven't left anyone out. God can't heal you if you're unwilling to forgive."

A thought pierced my side like a shard of glass. I had not forgiven God for Austin's death. My mind argued, *But God didn't take Austin. Sin did.*

The Spirit said, *But you're angry with God for not protecting your son.*

I said, *I have no right to be mad at God. How can I presume to forgive God when Austin was His in the first place? I didn't even have a right to him.*

The Spirit said, *Yes, your mind and your soul know, but your spirit still holds this against God. You need to forgive Him.*

"Repeat after me," Jeremy said.

I yielded. *Okay! I will say it.* The words fell painfully, slowly from my lips, like scabs from old wounds. "I forgive You, God, for not protecting Austin from the drunk driver."

Tears flooded my eyes and trickled down my cheeks. Despite all my effort not to blame God, I still had been angry with Him. My theological training, my Christian upbringing, my logic—all these things—taught me the spiritually correct responses to losing a son, but I still held this offense against God. I had allowed the enemy to rob me, not only of my son, but also of my joy in the Lord, my relationship with God, and a fulfilling relationship with my wife, family, and friends.

After the message and for the third time that week, I joined the thousands of others standing at the red lines to wait for prayer. A man my age approached and began praying for me. After he said a few things that really didn't hit the mark, I decided to tell him straight away what my problem was. I told him that I was still mourning my son and that I needed God to heal me. He embraced me as he prayed for God to heal me. I left, still not feeling that God had healed me. Lea could tell from the look on my face that my healing had not come.

"If Carol Arnott prayed for you," Lea said, "God would heal you." The tone in her voice was without hope. Carol had prayed for Lea in Dallas three years earlier at Spread the Fire, and Lea experienced a spiritual breakthrough.

The next morning, we attended the Sunday worship service. Jeremy led the praise time. Before the sermon, a woman gave a lengthy testimony about how bitter she had become when Pastor John Arnott and his wife, Carol, had not prayed over her barrenness a year earlier, even though she had gone forward several times. Eventually, God blessed her with a baby. Then, Pastor Arnott asked for people to come forward who wanted prayer for barrenness.

Lea looked at me. "Do you want to go up?"

"But we're old!" I said.

"Is this pride?"

I knew she was right. "Let's go."

We went forward for prayer. We stood in front with young parents who longed for the joy of rearing children, a privilege I continued to enjoy.

As John Arnott prayed for us, I stood there with my eyes closed. When I heard a woman praying for me, I fell to the floor on my back. "God," she said, "take away his grief and pain and fill him with joy."

As these words were spoken over me, God began removing the pain of death and loss from my heart. I lay there joyfully drenched in the presence and love of God.

Jeremy and the worship team began to sing "We Will Dance," Austin's favorite praise song. As the words about golden streets resounded over me, I realized that God was making a mockery of death. I pictured the tombstone over Austin's grave with the words, HE IS DANCING ON STREETS THAT ARE GOLDEN.

I heard these words in my spirit: *See, your son isn't rotting in a grave. He really is dancing on streets that are golden. God is mocking death. Your son is there!*

Happiness flooded my heart. Lea said my mouth gaped open in a wide smile as peace and joy soaked me. Before we got up from the floor, Lea and I looked at each other and laughed.

The festival had finally become one of joy for us. Reluctantly, we left the church for our campsite to prepare for our departure. But this time, I was determined to attend the evening service as well.

Connie Sinnott, the one I had been so critical of the night before, passed by to pray fervently over us. After about forty minutes of praying by faithful ministry team members, the Spirit of God overwhelmed me. In the presence of our awesome God, my physical being could not remain still. My arms and hands moved rapidly from side to side in front of my bowed head.

My head shook violently for several minutes. It seemed as if my arms were demonstrating the prophetic words spoken by the woman who was praying for both of us. Chopping movements of my hands responded to words that spoke of breaking strongholds in my life.

Lea couldn't focus on what the woman was praying over her, because she was basking in the joy of what God was doing in my life. The woman did say to Lea, "I see you as a Mary who leaves her own pain to minister to others. Your nourishment comes from ministering to the hurts of others." Lea remembered how God had pronounced the same word to her at Shady Grove.

Yes, God delivered me from grief, from sorrow, from places in my life where the enemy had created strongholds. God had even chosen, in His grace, to give us gold to confirm what He had done in spiritual places. For the first time, I embraced my son's admonition: "Dad, this life will be over soon. It's not real. Eternity is forever."

At last I was happy. At last I was free. I will dance with Austin and Jesus on streets that are golden.

Mitch Land *served under the International Mission Board of the Southern Baptist Convention from 1975 to 1990. The Lands spent more* *than twelve years in French Africa where Land was Director of Baptist Publications for the French speaking countries of the continent. Land is the Dean of Media and Worship Arts at The King's University. His wife and mother of Austin is Lea Land, retired principal. They have four children, 21 grandchildren, and one great granddaughter.*

Thoughts to Ponder
from Loss of a Child

1. God comforts those who are grieving.

2. We must forgive God if we harbor any resentment against Him.

3. All who have assurance of eternity will dance in Heaven.

Do you need to forgive God?

He will wipe every tear from their eyes. There will be no more death or mourning or crying or pain, for the old order of things has passed away. — Revelation 21:4

Are you a 10?

by Sharon Newton

On a scale of 1 to 10, how rich and satisfying would you say
your life is? Before you determine what your answer is, let me
tell you what I don't mean by rich and satisfying.

I don't mean:

- How much money you make or how much money you
  have.
- How impressive or how important your job is.
- What neighborhood you live in; how nice your house is.
- What car you drive.
- How well you dress or how nice you look.
- How well-educated you are; how many degrees you have.
- How perfect your family *seems*.

So what do I mean by rich and satisfying? When you
disregard all those things we always *thought* mattered most, you
should ask yourself these questions:

- Do I have genuine peace of mind?
- Do I have a sense of contentment with my life overall?
- Is my life meaningful and fulfilling?
- Do I know what my purpose is for being on this earth
  and am I achieving it?
- Do I look forward to the future with hope and
  anticipation?

These are the questions that will help you determine whether
your life is truly rich and satisfying.

Several years ago, if someone had asked me how rich and
satisfying my life was, on a scale of 1 to 10, I would have said 0,
or 2 at the most.

On the outside, I looked like the picture of success, a 9 or 10.
I was just finishing a large corporation's three-year international
assignment in London, England—the job I had dreamed about
since high school. I was making lots of money. I was financially
well-prepared for the future, enjoying an affluent lifestyle

traveling around the world for business and pleasure. And I had an active social life.

On the inside, I was empty.

I was externally rich but internally poor. I had everything and nothing at the same time. Maybe you've known a time when you felt that way.

By the time I was thirty-three, I had achieved every goal I had set for myself, yet my life lacked fulfillment. With a meaningless life void of purpose, success had failed me.

Yes, I could have set more goals. I could have begun new pursuits. But from what I had already experienced, I knew that was not the answer. Those new goals and new pursuits would have been nothing but mere time-fillers. Nothing on Earth could fill the emptiness inside of me. Not money or possessions. Not position or relationships. Not busyness. *Nothing!*

I couldn't go on living this way.

Many have experienced what it's like to be rich with money and possessions, yet feel empty and hopeless on the inside. If areas of your life are dry and barren, you're not alone. Many are struggling with their finances, health, career, marriage, or other relationships, looking to fill the void.

Having grown up in a home where the family went to church regularly, I was familiar with Christian teachings. But I had no real relationship with Jesus. My grandfather was a pastor, and throughout my life, I witnessed the close relationship he had with the Lord. Desperate and with nowhere else to turn, I decided to take a chance and try this God Who had been such an important part of my grandfather's life.

One Sunday morning after I returned to the United States, I went to church and walked to the front during the altar call. I barely noticed the crowd of people who had also come forward. I was determined to get in touch with the living God. I prayed fervently and gave Him control of my life. When I left, I was at peace, utterly confident that He had heard me. I had entered into a new relationship with Him.

Within only a few days, it became clear that I was to make others aware of what the Lord had done for me. So I volunteered my Saturdays at a resource center that provided assistance to the homeless and to people who needed help getting back on their feet. I shared with them how God loved them and sent His Son Jesus so they could find forgiveness and a new life through Him. Unfortunately, after a few months, that facility closed on Saturdays.

Confident that the Lord had another assignment for me, I prayed and kept my eyes open for other opportunities. Three months later, at a secular fraternity and sorority event, I had a conversation about the Lord with a man sitting next to me. He worked in a halfway house, a residential facility for men and women who were transitioning from prison back into society. I asked if they needed any volunteers, and he said they needed someone to teach a Bible study. Shortly thereafter, I met with the director of the facility, and the rest is history. Every week for the last twenty-six years, I have been teaching and counseling there. I also teach a monthly Bible study at a maximum security prison for men.

The Bible says those in Christ are a new creation. I have been depending on the Lord for almost three decades, and I can tell you that, beyond a shadow of a doubt, I have been changed into a new person. In no way do I resemble the woman who was once empty, purposeless, and searching for fulfillment—looking for meaning in life in all the wrong places. Now, I have a relationship with the Lord that is deeply gratifying. I would not trade it for anything in this world. Why? Because I know He cares about everything that concerns me.

- He ensures that all my needs are met, not just physical or material needs, but the internal needs of my soul and spirit.
- He gives me guidance to make wise decisions that bring His intended results.
- He protects me and everything that belongs to me.
- He warns me when I am about to say or do something that would displease Him so that I can refrain from it.
- He gives my life meaning and purpose by making clear what He put me on this earth to do.
- He gives me a deep sense of contentment with hope for the future.
- He fills that empty space inside of me with Himself.

- He makes my life rich and satisfying.

If someone were to ask how rich and satisfying my life is today, I would say without hesitation, "I'm an 8 on the way to 10."

Sharon Newton is originally from Chicago and is an author, professional speaker, and biblical counselor. She has taught and counseled residents of prisons and halfway houses for more than twenty years. Her goal is to provide others with an understanding of the Word of God, which enables them to develop an intimate relationship with the Lord. Sharon's book, a teaching novel, is called Bitter Cup, Sweet Aftertaste— Lessons from the Wilderness. *The book also has a companion study guide. Sharon lives in Dallas, Texas.*

Thoughts to Ponder
from Are you a 10?

1. Unrest comes when we are not where God wants us to be.

2. Our Creator desires a satisfying life for us.

3. God can lead us to our ultimate calling.

On a scale of 1 to 10, how rich and satisfying is your life?

Therefore, if anyone is in Christ, the new creation has come: The old has gone, the new is here! — 2 Corinthians 5:17

Silent Strength
by Renee Fowler Hornbuckle

When building a home, a solid foundation is important. It doesn't matter how beautiful the house is on the outside. If the structure is not sound from the bottom up, it won't withstand the pounding of external elements over the years.

Life is a lot like that. Thanks to a strong foundation, I was able to weather trials that I never dreamed I would face. I had a wonderful upbringing in a solid family with good morals and strong values. We were encouraged to be contributing citizens to society. My family believed in setting and achieving goals. This was a good foundation for me to build success in whatever I put my heart and mind to achieve. Life was good, and everything seemed to be on track for my life. High school graduation. College graduation. Successful career.

During my young adult years, my life took an unexpected turn. I was a bright and shining young college student with a great future. Mesmerized by the campus, I was influenced by the attention and affirmation of others.

I met this wonderful, good-looking top athlete on campus, and I was excited. I should have known something was up when his ex-girlfriend approached me, warning me to be careful. I paid no attention, reasoning that she was just jealous. I felt I could be successful and handle this relationship where she had failed.

Five years later, I was still in this relationship, well-acquainted with the world of control and manipulation. I should have paid attention to the signs, but I did not. I was in love. I also did not want people to know what I had endured. I was ashamed and in a state of emotional upheaval.

Through those years, I had to ask, *Have I been suffering?* After all, he had not abused me physically. But there had been so many mind games, emotional swings, and verbal abuses. He did everything he could to control and manipulate me. This up-and-down roller-coaster relationship took away the joy in my life. My parents had cautioned me to stay away from men like him, and now I knew I wasn't comfortable with this kind of life. I was suffering and alone, silently enduring the pain while wearing a happy-face mask.

On the day I decided to end our relationship, I shared my feelings. He became angry and thrust his fist through the wall in an uncontrollable rage. I was afraid. Of course, he apologized. He told me he would never do that again. But something inside me said, *Next time it will be you.* I stood my ground and called off the relationship.

For a while, he stayed away. Then I started seeing him show up where I was, glaring at me from across the room, the restaurant, or the mall. I could not believe he was stalking me. How could this be?

One day at a friend's house, the door flew off the hinges. Literally. My ex-boyfriend had kicked the door in to get to me. My friend pulled out a gun. I thought, *This is it! No one should have to live this way.* I had been in this abusive relationship for five years, and he still wanted to control my life. It was time for me to move on.

Too ashamed to tell my family or friends what I had been going through, I secretly quit my job and moved to Texas. Think about that—leaving and never telling a soul. To get away from a crazy person, I made a major geographical move to start a new life. I made sure I moved far enough away that he could not threaten me again.

I liked Texas and landed a great job. After one month, my father and my grandmother died. The grief was overwhelming. I took time off from my job and went to Arkansas to bury my father, then went to North Carolina to bury my grandmother. I dug deep for inner strength to help my family get through this difficult time. Once again, I faced a major decision. My first instinct was to remain in Arkansas to be near my mother, but we decided it would be best for me to pursue my dreams. For the next two years, I focused on advancing my career in Texas.

Life could not have been better. I was a young, successful corporate woman climbing the ladder to success. Still, I felt empty inside. This void caused me to do some deep soul-searching. I'm so thankful for that empty feeling, because after years of searching, I finally found what I was looking for—a right relationship with Jesus Christ.

58

I realized that there was more to life than just wild partying and making money. I wanted more out of life, and I knew I had more to give. But in order to get more, I needed a total makeover of who I had become. So I turned to God.

I had grown up with an awareness of God, but I never had a *right* relationship with Him. I was fully aware that a personal relationship with Jesus was what I needed to get my life on the right path.

I decided to seek out a church. I found the spiritual environment I had been raised in, where I was most comfortable. It had been a stable and consistent part of my upbringing.

When I surrendered my life to the lordship of Jesus, I eagerly developed an authentic personal relationship with Him. I became a true disciple and learner of the Bible. I proudly made the commitment to boldly share the gospel with others. I was on top of the world.

My co-workers were the first to notice the transition in my life. I no longer attended happy hour but invited them to attend an even happier hour—Bible study.

In pursuit of my positive life transition, I met a single man, who was leading the Bible study I attended. His ability to teach the Word of God was astounding. I was easily impressed by this man who appeared to be everything I desired. He had potential and big plans. He also treated me like a queen.

Our courtship was brief. After all, we were both active Christians and did not want to fall into sin. But once again, troublesome signs emerged. I heard that he had been married before. I decided it was probably no big deal. But when I asked, no one would discuss his marriage. Instead of pulling back, I overlooked the odd responses and thought, *Well, I won't worry about it.*

A few months later, we were married. I was totally committed to the relationship, and no one could have told me that he wasn't who he claimed to be. After all, I met him at church, and he was teaching a Bible study. As he had done while we were dating, he treated me like a queen and worked hard to give me everything my heart desired.

When swept into a whimsical world of romance with the

"perfect" man, it is hard to be objective. By all external indications, we were the picture-perfect family: A strong man, a smart woman, and three wonderful children. We had everything that displayed success: a beautiful home, luxury cars, money, and influence.

In 2005, my husband of seventeen years and co-founder of our church was accused of drugging and sexually assaulting female church members. He faced a separate charge after the police found drugs and a glass pipe in his car.

During the months that followed, I supported my husband amid these horrific attacks, even though everything else around us was falling apart. We even had press conferences, which I reluctantly participated in, because I had no idea what the truth was.

This ordeal became a headliner on national news. I was shocked. This was no laughing matter. It was life-shattering.

In 2012, as I began to reclaim my life, I knew this secret had to be revealed. How did I allow myself to end up in this situation? Our lives had taken off at a fast pace, and we rapidly rose to the top as a successful couple. I had great zeal in trying to be a godly pastor's wife. The responsibility of children, ministry, and other duties that came with being a public figure consumed me.

I got busy. I didn't slow down. I overlooked many things. I didn't fully comprehend how drastically things had changed. You would think that once someone has experienced manipulation and control that they would not buy into it again. However, it is often difficult to discern—this time packaged as charismatic and suave, with the promise of a fairy-tale life. I believed so strongly in everything about our relationship, I did not see that a part of me was being taken away.

Over the years, my husband's manipulation slowly changed. It started out as manipulation, then became more controlling, and finally turned to isolation and abandonment. Verbal, emotional, and mental suffering became the norm.

We can become so enamored by a relationship that we overlook the negatives. We get too close and are unable to see things for what they really are. I was too close to see the patterns of behavior that were being used against me to maintain absolute control.

Still, I ignored the issues and prayed things would change. Finally, I realized how dangerous things had become. On one occasion, I entered our bathroom, only to be backhanded and knocked into a tub full of water. I had just walked in from preaching and was fully dressed. Now, I was soaking wet. I thought, *This is enough!*

He thought I had disclosed his behavior and personal business to some of his accountability partners. I had not spoken with anyone. He was paranoid. The emotional and verbal abuse had finally reached its intensity in physical abuse. Still again, I remained silent.

As the years progressed, my husband changed for the worse. And the worse he got, the more I ignored the changes, mostly so I could keep the peace within the relationship and be the "good wife." I was suffering. I grew numb. I stopped feeling the pain. I tolerated the intolerable to keep peace.

The mistake I made was to never properly report the abuse to the authorities. Why? These records become public, and who wants everyone to know what is going on in their household?

Why am I coming forward now? Because I believe this is the appointed time that God has called me to share my story. I am one who now has the strength to stand and take this platform. My years of silence have been well-spent in the presence of God—healing, reflecting, resolving, forgiving, rebuilding, and coming to the place of peace. I hope breaking my silence helps you. I want others to know my journey, the lessons I learned, and how God brought me through.

Why don't we expose these silent issues in our lives? For me, it was fear, shame, and embarrassment. Thoughts like, *I should not be here. I'm smarter than this.* I endured verbal, emotional, mental, and physical abuse. Initially, I tried to minimize the physical abuse, but abuse is abuse. I finally got to the place where I was forced out of my denial. There comes a time when you must make a choice to open your eyes, look at the situation for what it is, and either come out or continue to live in denial. Finally, something snapped me out of the denial.

I want you to know that the way I made it through was by relying on God. My source of strength and courage came totally from God. By taking God's principles and applying them, you can turn things around. My motto was, face what's in front of you, not what's behind.

I took practical steps in finding the right kind of support to make positive change in my life:

- Spiritually, from the Word and spiritual counsel.
- Emotionally, from counsel, family, and authentic friends.
- Financially, through family and friends, and/or agencies that provided aid through the transition.

Everything you need to overcome your situation is already inside. Just apply God's Word. Just do it. With the greater source—God—nothing is impossible. Jesus said, "With man this is impossible, but not with God; all things are possible with God" (Mark 10:27).

To make a problem go away, you can't sit back and pretend it doesn't exist. You can't stay in denial. You must confront where you are. To those of us who profess to be Christians, God's Word is clear on what we must do. We must trust Him to see us through. If your life seems bent out of shape, may you find these words comforting: "Trust in the Lord with all your heart and lean not on your own understanding; in all your ways submit to him, and he will make your paths straight" (Proverbs 3: 5–6).

If you're facing a crisis, it is my hope that you find hope. I pray that you learn to walk the path of rebuilding your life on the strongest foundation: Jesus Christ.

Dr. Renee Fowler Hornbuckle *is a senior pastor, a community leader and advocate, a best-selling author, international speaker, Founder of the Life Empowerment Training and Development Institute, and CEO of InSight Consulting and the Phoenix Firm, LLC. She's also the Founder of Rachel's House, a transitional living home for women and families in crisis. In addition, she founded Women of Influence, Inc. and Destiny Empowerment Community Enterprises, Inc.*

Thoughts to Ponder
from Silent Strength

1. With a strong foundation, you can weather any storm.

2. God never intended us to suffer in silence.

3. Applying the Word of God to your life is one way to rebuild your foundation.

When have you suffered in silence?

For no one can lay any foundation other than the one already laid, which is Jesus Christ — 1 Corinthians 3:11

Was it Luck?

by Annie Lee

It was my thirtieth birthday. My husband offered to take me to breakfast anywhere I wanted before he flew to London on business. I chose a lovely hotel in Tarrytown, New York, overlooking the Hudson River. At breakfast, there were no flowers or brightly wrapped birthday packages. Instead, my husband said he wanted a legal separation, required in New York for an uncontested divorce.

Happy birthday to me.

I felt like I had been punched in the gut and kicked to the curb. He took me home, dropped me off, and left town. I fell apart. The bottom had just fallen out of my life.

Everything *seemed* to be going well. I had a great job. We had just bought our first house. I was happy. I thought *he* was happy and everything was good. I must have missed all the red flags. Now, my life was spinning out of control. I was alone and devastated. I confided in a few close friends, who told me I was well to be rid of him. Their advice didn't help. My heart was broken.

My mother's family had boycotted my wedding on religious grounds. There would be no sympathy there. My mother was no longer speaking to me, because I missed my grandfather's funeral in order to avoid her family. I felt isolated, not understood, and rejected.

I had to arrange selling the house, have our respective divided belongings moved, and find an apartment. To add insult to injury, one day on the walk home from the train station, my purse was snatched. We lived where three towns converged, and all the police got involved in trying to nab the thief. One officer showed me mug shots. Another officer rode me around the local streets, hoping I might spot the thief. I burst into tears. I felt like the last straw had fallen on my broken life.

"He didn't hurt you lady, did he?" he said.

"No," I said, "He didn't hurt me."

The competition for apartments in New York was fierce. However, I found a place. I just couldn't pull the trigger. My mind was muddled. The agent was astounded. He said there would be one more coming up in a month, and I should jump on it. I did. I couldn't believe my luck—a pre-war one-bedroom apartment with dining room, oak floors, ten-foot ceilings, fireplace, and picture frame molding, all for $300 a month— unheard of. I should have been leaping over-the-moon with joy, except now I was afraid to live alone.

I had a responsible full-time job as a paralegal for the International Law Division of a Fortune 500 company. However, I couldn't eat or sleep, and I was losing weight. I watched movies on television all night long. At 6:00 a.m., I showered and dressed, took the train into Grand Central Station, walked to my office on Park Avenue, and returned at night to my lonely apartment, my empty refrigerator, and the TV.

At work, I pretended that everything was fine. I told no one anything.

When my mentor at work retired after forty-seven years with the company, all the air got sucked out of my lungs. It wasn't because she was leaving, but because she had worked there more years than I had been alive. Would this be me? Was this all there was? Overnight, my dream job began to feel like a prison, and I wanted to break out.

I made some new friends at my apartment complex, all of whom worked for various airlines. They had lots of problems of their own and were into recreational activities that were new to me, like smoking pot and going to psychics, astrologers, and palm readers, none of which seemed to make them happy people. I tried it all anyway. Harmless diversions, right? But one day, I had the strangest foreboding, a sense of something sinister and evil. The thought was so strong that I realized, if evil was a real thing, God must be real too. I asked everyone I met about their religion—what they believed, what they were taught, and if they went to church. I didn't know what I was searching for, but everyone seemed happy to talk to me. Something was missing from my life, and I thought maybe it was God.

One afternoon after a call from my soon-to-be ex, I was very upset. Alone in my living room, I experienced a sharp pain in my chest that spread to my back, causing me to double over.

Thinking I was having a heart attack, I was scared. Down on the carpet, I cried, "Oh God, if You don't help me, I'm going to die." The pain stopped immediately. Amazing. What had happened? I thought it was some kind of primal scream, and that I did it. Why did I cry to God?—a God I didn't even know. Could God have heard me? Did God do it? I didn't tell anyone and forgot about it.

My not sleeping or eating had an effect on my thinking and behavior. When people remarked about my weight loss, I denied it, even though I was altering all my suits to make them fit. I had pains in my chest and in all my joints. I told my sympathetic General Practitioner that I had walking pneumonia and needed an x-ray, which he knew I did not. He said I looked "so put together"—my clothes, hair, makeup. But I was so "out of my mind" that he wanted me to see a psychiatrist. I refused. He then asked me an important question, one that had never occurred to me: *How long did I think I could live without eating or sleeping?*

I was going to die. I was now down to 102 lbs. That was a big wake-up call.

He told me to pour spicy barbecue sauce on everything to help me smell again, to taste and start eating again. He prescribed 5 mg of Valium each night so I could get four hours of sleep. It worked. He was going through a divorce and understood my pain. His kindness and empathy really impressed me. I felt like I was in good hands, and I needed that.

Eight months later, I woke up to the sun shining. I had slept through the night and no longer needed meds. I was also gaining weight. I was going to live.

My apartment went condo, and I was able to buy at a resident's discount. I put my renewed energy into remodeling and decorating. I hired a carpenter and sewed drapes. I loved being able to buy stuff without having to ask permission. I felt empowered and self-sufficient.

Many of my new friends were transferring out-of-state. I couldn't understand why anyone would want to leave. New York City had everything: theater, opera, ballet, and great museums. Why would anyone leave? It was all I knew. Then, again, I had that thought: *Was this all there is?—my job, my condo, my so-called life-style and status, diversions, acquiring more things. Was this what life was about?*

Maybe I should look for another job and move out-of-state as well. I could broaden my horizons. I prayed again to the God I did not know, and He seemed to answer me through a Job Counselor ad in the *New York Times* classified. It just jumped out at me. I made an appointment. This led to an interview with an insurance company for an eighteen-month training job for sales management. I would then be transferred somewhere yet to be determined. I accepted an offer, even though my job counselor advised me that sales was not for me. I knew he was right, but I felt I should take it anyway.

I bought a car, moved to New Jersey, and leased out my condo, all within the month. Somehow all the logistics aligned themselves and fell into place effortlessly. I began to feel that my life was no longer out of control—just not in *my* control. Something or someone had taken control of my circumstances—my condo, my doctor, this job—all these good things. I did not know how to explain this new good fortune. I called it good luck.

I did well during the months of training and was proud of myself. I was self-sufficient, independent, and confident—feeling very "lucky." Time to be relocated. I was offered Minneapolis, a great city and a great opportunity. New Jersey was cold, but Minneapolis was even colder. I said no. My first choice was Dallas, where I had visited twice in January on a recruiting trip, in mild weather. There was no opening in Dallas. Then, as "luck" would have it, there was an opening, so my boss and I headed to Houston for my interview. He asked how I knew about Dallas. I didn't know. I was not the one writing the script for my life. God was—the God I had yet to meet. Maybe I'd meet Him in Dallas.

I got the job, as well as an all-expenses-paid house-hunting trip and an executive move package. However, before I left New York, there was something very important that I felt compelled to do, even though I had some fear. I had to try to reconcile with my parents.

I wrote a letter, then made a phone call and arranged a visit. We agreed to start on the road to reconciliation and to healing our eight-year rift. From the moment I picked up the pen to when I picked up the phone, this too seemed to be orchestrated for me. I did the right thing. For the first time in a long time, I felt joy.

Many transplants to Texas like to say, "I wasn't born in Texas, but I got here as soon as I could." I say, "God got me here in His way and in His timing."

I found a patio home in Garland. The model I wanted was not available at first, and I was told to pray that someone's contract would fall through. I was naïve enough to do just that and got the model I wanted. Yet another prayer answered.

I worked long hours. I was team-building and teaching, even on the weekends. Then I went on sales calls with my recruits at night. I learned how to navigate the entire city. I also learned that my manager did not want a woman in this job. However, I didn't blink when he said that. He did. Within a year, he transferred back to Louisiana, and his next in command became my new boss. Instead of being better, I went from the frying pan into the fire.

I did two things that I would never do again: I did not pray to God, the One I still did not know. And I quit without having another job. I was sure I could find another one easily. This time I was too self-confident and independent. I began a learning curve on how to depend on God alone, not myself—to be God-confident, not self-confident. I still had no understanding of God. But I was beginning to get the point that I could not go it alone. John 15:5 says, "I am the vine and you are the branches. If you remain in me and I in you, you will bear much fruit; apart from me you can do nothing." I wanted to stay connected. I believed He was out there and had taken me from New York to Dallas. Now, I was unemployed. Would He still hear and answer my prayers? I really needed Him.

I made a friend who worked at the Texas Unemployment Commission office in Garland. He asked if I could type 75 wpm, which I could. He told me to show up at Oilwell Supply on Forest Lane. This division of U.S. Steel was not an easy company to get into, because they hired mostly relatives of employees. Openings were scarce, so he wished me luck. I got in—at entry level, working in the warehouse—starting over at the bottom, being humbled. However, I had a job and was really grateful.

During my five years at Oilwell, I was promoted four times. I was saved from multiple layoffs and an eventual merger. My second supervisor was the first of three benefactors, and he gave me the nickname "Lucky."

One year in July, my parents came to visit for a week during a prolonged heat wave. My car's air conditioning was not working. A friend let me borrow his car so I could take my parents to the Kimball Art Museum to see an exhibit of miniature portraits. They talked about that exhibit for years after. They liked my house and my new puppy. We were on good terms again.

On Sundays, I picked churches at random to visit. I was trying them all out, with no game plan. Some were welcoming, some decidedly unfriendly. Some were spooky, some downright scary. I never really listened to a message or learned anything. I was still clueless. I had not met God anywhere yet. Then one day, Emil, an elderly widower who lived two houses down, invited me to attend a service at his church the following weekend.

My life was about to change forever.

His church had been praying for me. That Sunday, I was introduced to the Bible. I was in awe. I had never read God's Word, so I bought my own Bible. A few weeks later, I heard a sermon about the Parable of the Prodigal Son from the New Testament book of Luke. A young man asked for his inheritance, left home, and squandered everything on reckless living. Penniless, without friends or food, he returned home to beg his father to hire him as a servant, because he was so ashamed. However, the father was watching for his return. On the day he saw him coming, he ran to him. Before his son could say anything, he hugged him and called for a robe, shoes, and a signet ring to be put on him. He completely restored him to his place in the family.

That was August 1, 1982, the day I got my greatest wake-up call. I realized that I was like that prodigal son. I was separated from my Father God, Who wanted me to be His child. All the lights went on in my head, and I finally got it. God was inviting me to be reconciled with Him, but like the prodigal, I first needed to ask forgiveness.

Through this sermon and these scriptures, I realized how deeply disappointing I must be to God. I was flawed, a person who didn't meet His perfect standards. I didn't measure up. Maybe I didn't know God, but He knew everything about me—all my unkind thoughts, my secrets, my temper fits, and my angry words. He knew how arrogant, self-centered, prideful, and selfish I could be. He knew I was prone to ridicule and sarcasm. My self-confidence and independence were not pleasing Him either. Labeling His goodness to me as "good luck" was an insult to Him.

Like the prodigal, I needed to humble myself, apologize, and repent. God wanted to forgive me all along. He had been drawing me to Him with His kindness and love. God was the One Who opened the right doors for me and directed my steps. He provided for me and protected me. All these good things came from Him. I then knew Who to thank for my so-called "luck" and to call it what it really was: God's goodness.

I was grateful that He got my attention by changing my circumstances. He worked through other people until I could learn enough to turn from the world's ways and choose His way. God was offering me a relationship. On this Sunday when I was thirty-seven, I said yes to God's invitation, and my life changed forever.

Happy, happy birthday to me.

Life is full of pitfalls and traps that can snare and blindside us when we make uninformed choices. Living life as a believer is not without suffering. I have grieved the loss of both my parents. I have had setbacks in my career and layoffs from jobs. Friends have turned on me. But heartaches and troubles don't rock my boat anymore, because God is a friend forever. He never leaves us nor forsakes us. He is faithful.

My circumstances can change, but through Christ, I have the ability to remain steady. I can bring all my cares and troubles to God. He hears my prayers, and He answers my prayers. I have His scriptures to guide me. I have His Spirit to counsel me. I have a moral compass and direction, and I am no longer just drifting.

Now I have a relationship with the God Whom I was praying

to. He has a plan for my life—an actual plan for my future. I am no longer clueless, without direction or without hope. I don't have to worry. I have real peace.

You can have a personal relationship with God too. He sent His Son Jesus to pay for our sin with His own life. Death is God's penalty for sin. Jesus paid that penalty for all mankind so every person can be free to choose a relationship with Him, to live with Him forever. This is why Jesus came to Earth, why He was born and why He died and was resurrected. Jesus did for us what we could not do for ourselves.

Our sins separated us from God. Jesus reconciled us to God. Will you make a choice to be reconciled with Him today? All you have to do is believe in Him and accept what He did for you. He will do the rest. Don't wait. Don't let your *luck* run out. Turn instead to God's goodness.

Today can be your birthday in Jesus, which will change your life forever.

Annie Lee *was born in New York City and transferred with her employer to Dallas Texas, where she has lived for 40 years. After retiring from corporate work as a paralegal, administrative assistant, and bookkeeper, she took a position with a ministry with the vision of seeking reconciliation and understanding between Christians and Messianic Jews. She is an active member of her Messianic Synagogue in Dallas and enjoys group Bible studies. Once a month she holds fellowship dinners for other single believers.*

Thoughts to Ponder
from Was it Luck?

1. Luck is fleeting. God's goodness is not.

2. God is waiting for all prodigals to return to Him.

3. We are designed to be connected to Jesus.

When did you realize that life was not about luck?

*If you declare with your mouth, "Jesus is Lord,"
and believe in your heart that God raised him from the dead,
you will be saved. — Romans 10:9*

Dreams from Above
by Loren Adair

Are you a dreamer?

Do you remember your dreams when you wake up in the morning? I've had very vivid dreams that I could soar through the air like a bird. I felt the struggle of running and flapping my arms to get up into the air. Once I was airborne, I was soaring over rooftops and across forests. It was beautiful. In one dream, my friends and I were being chased by a bear. No one was supposed to know that I could fly. I told them to run with me, and right when the bear was about to snatch us, I began to fly. By having them hold on and fly with me, I saved us in the nick of time. What a dream.

My childhood was what some people would call a dream. I was raised in a wonderful home, with parents who loved and encouraged me. My brother was six years older. Growing up in Dallas, I had a tremendous group of friends. I was involved in school, church, Young Life, music, school organizations, volunteer groups, and travel. Many people would call my life "charmed." My parents gave me a lot of confidence, because they believed in me and supported me.

From a young age, I enjoyed being with my mother. Some of my friends said they couldn't believe what a good relationship we had. They did not get along with their moms so easily. We had a lot of freedom in those days, because the world was not as dangerous a place as it is now. Some of my favorite childhood memories were leaving in the morning on my bicycle and being gone with friends all day, only to come home to eat and refuel to go back out again. I had a truly amazing and blessed childhood.

My parents took us to church and prayed with me at night. However, they did not talk with me about their faith or teach me much about the Bible. I thought they were from that generation of people who were more "private" about their faith. I watched my dad in church being deep in prayer and knew his faith was real, even if he didn't say very much. He was a strong and quiet person.

From my earliest memories, I desired to know God. I now know the Holy Spirit had planted that desire in me. I thought the people who were closest to God were nuns. While I was not Catholic, I dreamed of growing up to be a nun so I could be close to God. I had those feelings from age five to twelve.

In my youth, I thought I was Christian because I went to church and youth group and desired to know God. But one night, a friend of mine invited me to her church youth meeting in her home. For the first time, I heard that every person on Earth has sinned—doing things that are not pleasing to God. I learned that God is holy and cannot live around sin. He loves us and created us to have a relationship with Him, so He sent His one and only Son, Jesus, to live a perfect life and die on a cruel cross to pay the price for my wrongdoings. I only needed to receive this gift of salvation, believe that Jesus came and died for my sins, and confess to Him that I wanted Him to be my Lord and Savior. I was dumbfounded to learn that I did not have a relationship with God, so I went home that night and received Him as my Savior. I repeated the salvation prayer for several days, just to be sure He had heard me. I wanted to know with 100 percent certainty that I was a Christian, as I had always believed I was.

My faith journey has been a steady growth process throughout my life. I did not have one of those amazing transformations where I was an addict. Some visibly outward issue didn't require a radical change after I accepted Jesus. At one time, I thought I didn't really have much of a story to tell. Now I know that we all have a story, God's story, because He is at work in every one of us—like a potter molding his clay into a beautiful creation. I was changed from the inside out. Before I accepted Christ, I was all about myself and how my life could be great. I was focused on being popular, cool, and accepted by everyone. I was fearful, afraid of dying, and scared to be alone. God has been at work in me, and will continue until the day that I go to Heaven to live with Him eternally.

During my freshman year of college, I had a significant turning point. I began to question my faith and considered investigating other religions. One night while I was feeling extremely confused about the direction I should take, I cried out to God in my dorm room and asked Him to give me specific guidance for my future. The next day, as I was walking across the University of Texas campus, I saw an alumnus from my high school. She said, "Loren, I heard that you W.T. White girls were here at U.T., and I was hoping to start a Bible study with you." A feather could have knocked me over. What was the likelihood that I would run into her on this large campus? I believed this could not have been a coincidence. God had intervened. She discipled me for the next two years and got me into serving high school students in the Young Life organization. This was a great turning point for me as God turned my focus outward. He gave me a yearning to know Him more deeply, serve Him well, and tell others about the Good News of Jesus' love.

Another issue of mine that God had to work on was my fear of death. As a young person, I was afraid of dying, and now I know there is no reason to fear. God's perfect love casts out fear. The Bible says, "Do not be anxious about anything, but in every situation, by prayer and petition, with thanksgiving, present your requests to God. And the peace of God, which transcends all understanding, will guard your hearts and your minds in Christ Jesus" (Philippians 4:6-7). As sad and horrifying as my last four years have been, I can tell you that I now have a peace that could *only* come from God.

Spencer, my husband of thirty-five years, was diagnosed with esophageal cancer in 2015. Both he and my mother died in 2016, only seven months apart. They were my two best friends. Spencer was my life mate. I was devastated—sad and grief stricken. For a year and a half, he fought a very strong and courageous battle with cancer and died the day after Christmas. He was ready to be with Jesus and often said during his illness that "God has a plan." Closer to his death, he said Jesus needed him in Heaven for some special job. Spencer was completely at peace during his illness, because he knew he was going to his real home. This has brought me tremendous peace in dealing with his death.

We thought my mom had died of natural causes the previous May. She was ninety-one, but was very alive and vibrant, acting more like seventy. We were shocked to get the call from her senior living center that she had died in her sleep. However, that was not nearly as shocking as the call I received in April 2018. The Dallas police believed she had actually been murdered in her apartment by a serial killer. This sent us reeling. Exactly three years from the day of her death, her killer was indicted in Dallas for the murder of twelve elderly women. But thanks be to God that though "the thief comes to kill and destroy," Jesus Christ came to give eternal life, which cannot be taken away.

I have screamed and yelled and cried and mourned and questioned why this horrendous thing could have happened. At the same time that my husband was battling for his life, this man took the life of my other best friend, my mother. With only an earthly perspective on this, I would have gone to bed and not gotten up. The only explanation for the amazing peace and strength I had is that God lifted and carried me every single day. It's a strength I still have today.

I have a story, one of many, to share with you as an example of God's intimate, dear love for us. On the day of my husband's funeral in early January 2017, he was being buried at the National Cemetery in Dallas because he was a veteran. That morning, I was getting ready for the burial and memorial service. As I was putting on my jewelry, I decided not to wear my big clunky watch. I had a dressy watch that I could wear. I pulled it out of the jewelry box, but it wasn't working. I tried winding it, but it still wouldn't run. Since it was a quartz watch, I thought shaking might get it going. That didn't work either. Since I wouldn't have to look at my watch, I put it on anyway.

During the procession to the National Cemetery, the morning was freezing cold, an unusual sixteen degrees, so the veteran motorcycle group wasn't insured to escort us, but a couple of them did anyway. When we arrived at the cemetery, I was amazed. The rest of the veterans were standing at attention in the freezing cold, along with so many friends and family. It was a dear and amazing show of love.

We were sitting in the motorcade, waiting for our time to proceed, as the military is very precise about everything. All of a sudden, the driver of our vehicle said, "It's 11:03, time to pull out." I felt prompted to look at my watch, which was stopped— at 11:03. God poured out on my Spirit a flood of scripture. "Your eyes saw my unformed body; all the days ordained for me were written in your book before one of them came to be" (Psalm 139:16) He spoke into my spirit, *I have known this day from the beginning of time. I am right here beside you, and I will carry you every single day.* This is just one example of the intimacy of God Almighty, Who created every star in the sky and every hair on your head. His love for us is unfathomable.

God has sent many people to lift me up in the crises of both my husband's and my mother's deaths. Our three amazing children and their spouses, along with our grandchildren and other family and friends have held me close and supported me. God has provided the scriptures I needed to hear for each grief or hardship. From my earliest years, He has been preparing me to have a hunger for Him and for His Word, which has come back to me as I needed it in times of anguish. He has provided for my physical, emotional, and spiritual needs. He has helped me know that I am not alone, and He understands my incredible sadness. He watched His own Son die a horrific death on the cross, so He knows my pain. He cares about me. He cares about you as well.

God has not promised that life will be easy. We can trust Him even when we can't understand why things happen the way they do. You can tell Him everything, how much it hurts, how unfair it feels. Tell Him every heartache as well as every joy. I have screamed, groaned, cried, and laughed with God. His love for us is more than we can understand. He sent His own Son to die for us, because He wants a relationship with us. Listen, listen, listen. Don't just talk to God. Stop to hear what He is trying to tell you. Be still and ask Him. He will speak into your spirit, but you have to stop and listen.

He has been preparing my entire life for these times. I crave studying His Word and have been His student for forty-eight years. The Bible is the most profound and amazing book, packed full of wisdom with never a dull moment. We will never learn everything there is to know. The Bible is God's love story to us.

I received eternal life and a relationship with God because someone was willing to tell me the story of Jesus Christ. We can only understand God's love for us by hearing His story. Someone is out there who needs to hear mine, and someone is out there who needs to hear yours. They need to hear about God's love and forgiveness and the life He has given us. As my husband said, "God has a plan," and God wants us to be part of that plan.

If you have never received Christ as your Savior, don't wait. Do it now, even if you have questions. Pray this prayer: "God, thank You that You love me. I know that I have fallen short and have done things to separate me from You. Thank You for sending Your Son, Jesus, to die on the cross as payment for my sins. I know You are holy and loving and want a relationship with me. I accept Jesus as my Savior so I may spend eternity with You. Thank You for this life."

If you haven't already done so, get into a Christian community. We need one another to spur ourselves on. We need a sounding board—people to share life with, who will encourage us in the faith.

I have one more dream to share with you. In 2010, my husband, my youngest son, and I were driving home late at night from a special memorial service in College Station. Our middle child, who was in school there, called to check on us around midnight. He had been a participant in this special service. When he called, he awakened me from a dream I was having. In the dream everything was dark, except Jesus was standing in a white robe that was glowing. He was radiating a love that I could feel in the dream. There were no audible words, but He spoke into my spirit, saying, "I want people to know this love that I have for them. Tell people about My love." Ever since then, I have known this is what I have to do. God wants us to know this love, and He wants us to tell others about His love, eternal life, and relationship with Him.

He wants me to tell you that He loves you and wants you to love Him too.

Loren Adair *was raised in Dallas and went to the University of Texas at Austin, where she earned a degree in Interior Design. She married Spencer Adair in 1980, and was married almost 37 years before his death in 2016. Loren has three children, two of which are married, and four grandchildren. After working in the Interior Design field for ten years, Loren and her husband started Adair Printing & Promotions, Inc. in*

*1988, a company she still runs today. Loren loves volunteering with Roaring Lambs, needlework, reading, travel, and spending time with family and friends. Contact her at **LAdair@RoaringLambs.org**.*

Thoughts to Ponder
from Dreams from Above

1. God can use dreams to speak into your spirit.

2. Grief is never easy, but God will move you through it.

3. Put your faith in Jesus so He can direct your path.

How do you hear from God?

In the past God spoke to our ancestors through the prophets at many times and in various ways. — Hebrews 1:1

Walking Through the Fire
by Fran Caffey Sandin

Attendants wheeled a bleeding, unconscious teenage boy into the operating room of Parkland Hospital in Dallas, Texas, just after midnight. Another motorcycle accident. The operating-room team scurried about, tending to the boy's head and chest injuries, and multiple broken limbs. As a student nurse, my heart pounded with excitement as we worked fervently to save him. When our efforts failed, the doctor looked at me and said, "Come with me while I talk to the family."

Outside the double doors, the surgeon gently said, "I'm sorry. We did everything we could."

I watched the faces of the parents as their expressions changed from hopeful expectation to shock, disbelief, and finally tears. Their only son had died. I wanted to comfort them, but words stuck in my throat. I cried too, although I didn't fully comprehend their pain. Years later, I understood.

I recalled my grandmother's brief hospitalization during my childhood, when I was picking blackberries and peaches, and working at my grandpa's East Texas fruit stand. While visiting Ma at our small hospital, I observed a nurse whose white, crisp uniform, gracious smile, and professional manner caused me to think, *I'd like to be a nurse someday.* I never changed my mind. On his way to work in his mechanic shop, my father drove me to high school each day. My younger brother and sister were involved in their own activities. My mother, an excellent cook and homemaker, actively participated at our school and church.

During my senior year, I took the Betty Crocker Homemaker of Tomorrow written examination. To my great surprise and delight, I won for the state of Texas and received a scholarship, enough for me to attend Texas Woman's University College of Nursing.

While at Parkland Hospital during my sophomore year of student clinicals, a tall, handsome Swedish sophomore medical student introduced himself in the library and invited me for coffee. I accepted. We dated two years, graduated, and then married. I became Mrs. James Howard Sandin.

We were both financially challenged. Jim's dad died in an auto accident when he was a high school senior, so a scholarship enabled him to finish his undergraduate studies at Yale University prior to attending University of Texas Southwestern Medical School. He worked his way through. I sewed my wedding dress and made the crown for my veil out of pipe cleaners and pearls, all for less than $25.

We moved to Little Rock, Arkansas, where Jim completed a year of internship at the University Hospital, and I worked on the medical surgical unit. Jim served as a Captain in the Air Force for two years, the first in Cam Ranh Bay, South Viet Nam. I transferred to East Texas and worked at a hospital. When Jim returned, we moved to Tinker AFB in Oklahoma City. While there, Jim completed a four-year residency in urology at the OU Medical Center, and our first two children, Steve and Angie, were born. We then moved to Greenville, Texas, where Jim began his urology solo practice in their new hospital. One year later, our son, Jeffrey, was born. As a full-time mom of three preschoolers, my days were filled with a variety of smiles, laughter, and sometimes a few tears.

One evening when I attended an evangelistic service at the Greenville Municipal Auditorium, I didn't expect anything to happen to me, but it did. As the pastor preached about the prodigal son, the Lord touched my heart. I realized that *I had all of Jesus, but He did not have all of me.* That evening, I came home, placed myself on an imaginary altar, and said, "I am Yours— body, soul, and spirit. I want my life to honor You and bring glory to Your name." With renewed joy and excitement about the Bible and my time alone with God, I realized anew what Jesus had done for me. Hymns from my youth came alive in my spirit as I felt His amazing grace.

One day, a friend, prompted by the Holy Spirit, gave me a book to read: *Stewardship of Sorrow.* I didn't understand why, but I thanked her. One morning as I was at the kitchen sink, the Lord impressed me with the words: *You will soon go through a very dark valley, but don't be afraid. I will be with you.* I had no idea what would transpire.

At the age of seventeen months, our blonde, blue-eyed, vibrant toddler, Jeffrey, became ill with what we expected to be

82

a short-term viral illness. Before the days of the meningitis vaccine, many children between the ages of six months and three years were stricken. Sure enough, Jeffrey's diagnosis was Hemophilus Influenzae, type B, bacterial meningitis, the strain that attacks the brain and spinal cord. Our family maintained an optimistic vigil, but three days later, after a respiratory arrest, Jeffrey was placed on life-support. The next day, a pediatric neurologist and several attending physicians advised us to remove the respirator. Jeffrey's brain was no longer functioning. Hope for his recovery vanished.

When Jim and I saw Jeffrey's ashen, lifeless body in ICU, our spirits confirmed the report. We were no longer supporting life but prolonging death. Jim and I went to the hospital chapel, where we knelt and Jim prayed, "God, we pray You will use this for our good and for Your glory." With tearful anguish and sorrow, but also with a supernatural sense of peace, we stood beside our son's bed to pray and release him to his Maker.

Now I understood the agony of other families in their losses. While many friends and family lent their warm and loving support, I struggled to cope. Steve was five and Angie was three. Everything had happened so fast, my emotions could not catch up with reality. I wrestled with burning questions: *Is God punishing me? How can I conquer fear? Will I ever get over this? Does God answer prayer? Am I becoming bitter? How can God possibly use this experience for good?*

For several years, I asked the Lord to be my counselor and help me find answers to my concerns. It became a step-by-step process. There is no "drive through" instant recovery for grief. Burying a child is so unnatural—like placing a part of oneself in the grave. Searching for answers, I spent time in scriptures, prayer, and fellowship with other believers. I raised my spiritual antenna to capture any thread of truth or insight.

Two years later, I felt the Holy Spirit leading me to write a book that could help parents dealing with loss, who were probably asking the same questions that I was. I remembered 2 Corinthians 1:3–4 that says God comforts us so others can experience the same comfort He has given us. At that point, I argued with God. "I'm not a writer."

In my spirit, He said, *I Am.*

"But I don't know how to write a book."

He said, *I do.*

In response to His unrelenting tugs, I chose to exercise faith. My friend Nancy, an English teacher, helped me make an outline. We talked about my journey through grief, my questions, my memories of Jeffrey, and verses that had sustained me.

One day a week, after taking Steve and Angie to their school, I drove thirty minutes from our home to our rustic cabin on Lake Tawakoni and spent the day writing, typing, and crying. It took four years to develop a manuscript. When finished, I didn't know what to do, so I went to the public library, checked out a book, and followed directions on how to submit a manuscript. I didn't know how to evaluate the publishing houses, so I kept getting returns. Now and then, an editor included a sentence of encouragement. I left the manuscript in the drawer for months, because I didn't know what to do next.

Thankfully, the Lord provided a divine encourager, who suggested I attend a Christian writer's conference. After receiving good advice at the conference, I rewrote the manuscript. The following year, *eleven years* after I began writing and on the twenty-seventh submission, Tyndale published *See You Later, Jeffrey.* By then, I could talk about our loss without crying. On several occasions, I was invited to speak for various church groups, and I even had a few radio and television interviews.

My family was supportive. While I worked part-time in Jim's medical office, served as a church organist, and focused on Steve and Angie, I continued to attend writer's conferences, read, and work toward improving my writing skills. Jim supported me through it all. He even attended a writer's conference with me. We stayed in a college dormitory on the fourth floor. The elevators were not working on a very hot July day, but my 6'4" hubby trudged up the stairs, carrying our suitcases. With sweat on his brow, he made a second trip to pick up bedding. Jim never complained about anything, not even when his feet hung off the bunk bed in our doll-sized room. The Lord abundantly met my needs, even when learning about writing and publishing was tacked onto an already busy schedule.

Four years after publication of the Jeffrey book, I received a telephone call from my mother's neighbor, who lived an hour's drive east of us. Ruth said in almost a whisper, "Your mother needs you right now. Come immediately, and bring Jim."

I gasped. "What happened?"

"Just come as quickly as you can." She gave no explanation.

Shocked and shaking, I said, "We will."

Jim and I rearranged our day and drove to the brick, ranch-style country home. A sheriff's car occupied the circle driveway. When we rushed inside, the sound of my mother's cries confirmed my worst fear.

In a bout of depression, Dad had shot himself and died. The moment seemed surreal as my brother, sister, and I attempted to console Dad's sweet bride of fifty years, while feeling the pain and loss ourselves. A World War II veteran and a strong loving father, Daddy was under a doctor's care and taking medications. Suicide was so out of character for him, but we knew he had a strong faith and had made his peace with God. It was difficult to imagine he would not be with us on Earth, but this verse comforted me: "For I am convinced that neither death nor life, neither angels nor demons, neither the present nor the future, nor any powers, neither height nor depth, nor anything else in all creation, will be able to separate us from the love of God that is in Christ Jesus our Lord (Romans 8:38–39).

A week later, I lifted a very heavy child in the church nursery. Unfortunately, back pain resulted, and I spent time recovering— with the help of a physical therapist. So I was grieving my dad's death plus dealing with painful restrictions and emotional distress. I was weeping and asking, "God, where are You?" He seemed to have pulled down a dark shade.

God showed me where He was through His Word. The verses that helped me were:

- I am laid low in the dust; preserve my life according to your word (Psalm 119:25).
- My soul is weary with sorrow, strengthen me according to your word (Psalm 119:28).
- My comfort in my suffering is this: Your promise

preserves my life (Psalm 119:50).

I remembered John 16:33, which says we will have tribulation and trouble in this world, but take heart because Jesus has overcome the world. Gradually, I knew faith would see me through.

But Jim and I were not prepared for what happened next.

How does a young man in the prime of life deal with an incurable disease, loss of strength, the news that he cannot be a father, and the likelihood of a shortened life-span? Our son, Steve, had just completed his Master of Physical Therapy degree and was working at a hospital on his first professional job when he became ill, hospitalized with pneumonia. His doctor said, "Steve, I believe you have cystic fibrosis." *What?* Two positive sweat tests confirmed the diagnosis, and he began respiratory therapy that would be required for the rest of his life.

Jim and I were shocked. No one else in our family had the genetic disease. From 8 to 10 percent of cystic fibrosis (CF) patients are diagnosed in adulthood. Tests verified that truth for us. We had no idea we were carriers of the CF gene. Cystic fibrosis destroys the lungs by clogging them with thick secretions and causes other organs to malfunction because of the mal-distribution of cellular salt and water.

Digestion is also affected, so Steve began taking digestive enzymes. No cure is currently available for CF. As part of his physical therapy training, Steve had learned how to treat patients with CF, but he had no idea that he would become his own caregiver.

The shock of this news had barely become a reality when Steve almost died with renal failure due to IgA nephropathy, a separate autoimmune disease. Added to his respiratory treatments, he then needed three trips a week to the hemodialysis clinic. Still, he continued working part-time in home health physical therapy. After three years, he switched to peritoneal dialysis that allowed him to use a computerized machine at home, where he dialyzed at night. Finally, he did not have the strength to continue his profession, but he used his time for a home-based business and wrote and published two books based on God's Word, *Jesus Really Said It* and *Make the*

Right Choice.

Steve lived every day with hope. As a child, he had received Jesus as his Savior, and he continued growing in faith throughout his years. He prayed daily and believed God could completely heal him if it was His will. One day Steve said, "Mom, I know God can heal me, but if He doesn't heal me on Earth, I know I will be healed in Heaven." His healing came after much suffering at his last hospitalization, when irreversible complications of CF accelerated. At the age of 43, Steve moved peacefully to Heaven on Sept. 22, 2012.

Along the way, I read a booklet on *Grief* by the late Dr. Haddon Robinson. He used three words that helped me when once again as I traversed the death of a son: **CRISIS**, **CRUCIBLE**, and **CONSTRUCTION**. Because I experienced God's faithfulness following Jeffrey's death, I had been tested and knew He would be with me. I recalled the words of Shadrach, Meshach, and Abednego, when they said they would trust God *even if* He did not deliver them through the fire. When King Nebuchadnezzar looked inside the fiery furnace, he saw a fourth figure. Jesus was with them, and when they emerged, they did not even smell of smoke. I learned still more of God's faithfulness. What follows are some things I learned:

CRISIS

Two characteristics of the crisis phase are shock and denial. When a crisis hits, our first words are usually, "Oh no, it can't be," or, "I don't believe it." That's how I felt when my father died. That response is God's way of protecting us. God knows how much we can bear, and He allows us to gradually assimilate it. Otherwise, we would be overwhelmed. Weeping does not denote lack of faith. It's an important part of the grieving and healing process.

CRUCIBLE

A crucible is a container for melting ore. This fiery trial follows the initial crisis and is the most difficult, because it is characterized by questions, doubts, and guilt. Sometimes it lasts for several months, maybe longer, depending upon the person's disposition. We enter trials with various temperaments, personalities, previous life events, and responses. Each person's crucible is unique. An emotionally stable person may handle this phase more quickly than one whose emotional reserve is empty. However, regardless of a person's spirituality, he or she will "walk through the fire" on the way to recovery.

What are some typical reactions? Anger, fear, loneliness, blame, or physical problems such as heart palpitations, insomnia, and dizziness. Other stress symptoms may be difficult to diagnose. *The crucible phase is a danger zone.* Trials test our concept of God, and since our culture advertises that we have a right to be happy, healthy, and satisfied, we may be tempted to question the Lord and say, "If You allow distress, then do You really care or even exist?" That is why it is so important for us to saturate ourselves with scriptures during the good times. Then the Holy Spirit will use those verses as a healing balm and a balancing beam when struggles come.

Instead of facing the crucible head-on and dealing with it, some people want an anesthetic. They try to numb the pain with drugs, alcohol, or overeating. Adjustment to change is not easy, but we find reassurance in God's words to Paul: "My grace is sufficient for you" (2 Corinthians 12:9).

I got through the crucible by believing that God is working and accomplishing His purpose, even though I did not understand. I concentrated on being thankful—thankful that we had Jeffrey for seventeen months, thankful for my Dad's good qualities, and thankful for Steve's faith and perseverance through suffering. I went to church even if I didn't feel like it. I talked through my feelings with a trusted friend. When I prayed, I was honest with God. I remembered a quote from the late Dr. Joseph Bayly: "Never forget in the darkness what you have learned in the light." I found out that if I would do the right thing and take the next step, feelings would follow.

CONSTRUCTION

Finally. Recovery of full emotional energy takes time. We struggle to take three steps forward and fall two steps backward. But at last, a time emerges when our thoughts are not always focused on the loss. Do we forget the person we loved? No, but our memories of them are centered on the happy times we had, not so much on the death.

As healing continues, we once more direct our attention to ways we can honor God. One of the goals of the construction phase is to develop new interests and patterns not closely linked with the past. Some people have taken up painting, volunteer work, nursing home ministries, and other activities. The options are unlimited. For me, it was writing, and my desire to help other families. God took me step-by-step and opened the way for *See You Later, Jeffrey* to be published. Our story is touching people I would ordinarily never meet. It has been translated into Russian, and it ministers to families in the Ukraine and Germany.

Suggestions for the construction phase include: think about some positive aspect of your loved one (joyfulness, honesty, courage, etc.) and incorporate it into your life so a characteristic of the person lives on in you. Reach out and serve others according to your ability. Forgive whatever needs to be forgiven and accept God's grace. Plan and look forward to something in the future.

When dealing with loss, it is important to remember that "this, too, shall pass." Life is a dynamic drama of change. Each day is a special gift from God. No other day will be exactly like it. That is why we must make the best of each opportunity—to love, to encourage, and to come alongside to uplift one another. Sometimes I'm the one helping. At other times, I am the one being helped.

No matter what kind of fire we are going through, how bad we feel, or how grim our circumstances are, Christ is our hope. The Lord saved Shadrach, Meshach, and Abednego. He was with them through the fire. It is possible to zig-zag our way to construction and know we will experience brighter days because Jesus is already there.

A thankful heart is the key to joy, fruitful living, and peace. Jim and I are so thankful for the children God gave us, and we thank Him for the precious time we had with Jeffrey and with Steve. Our beautiful daughter, Angie, married a wonderful man, and they have given us two fabulous granddaughters and a special grandson, who reminded us of Jeffrey when he was young. Now a teenager, he displays some of Steve's admirable characteristics. Isn't that just like our wonderful God? We are greatly blessed.

Fran Caffey Sandin, *a retired nurse, is the author of* See You Later, Jeffrey, *and* Touching the Clouds: True Stories to Strengthen Your Faith. *She has contributed to other books and magazines. Fran and her physician-husband, Jim, are active in their church in Greenville, Texas. They are parents of a beautiful daughter and son-in-law, whose three wonderful children are a grandparent's dream. The Sandins have two sons awaiting them in Heaven. Fran enjoys Community Bible Study, flower arranging, hostessing, walking, reading, traveling, piano, and organ playing. She has fun with grand-dog puppies, Daisy and Lilly. Visit her website at* **FranSandin.com**.

Thoughts to Ponder
from Walking Through the Fire

1. God is always with us in the fire.

2. There are often opportunities to comfort others as God has comforted us.

3. It's okay to grieve.

When has God walked with you through a fire?

My soul is weary with sorrow; strengthen me according to your word. — Psalm 119:28

Rollercoaster

by Mandy Gaeth

Who likes rollercoasters? Buckle up!

We are taking a wild ride through the first forty-five years of my life as Mandy Close. We'll hit extreme highs, then dive to devastating lows—and do it all over again. The sovereignty of God and His power alone, will bring us to a screeching halt. What then?

I grew up Down Under in the beautiful beach towns along the east coast of Australia. My family did not attend church and had no knowledge or regard for God. Alcohol is a huge problem in Australia. By age five, both my parents were out-of-control raging alcoholics. They fought wildly when intoxicated and hated each other. Therefore, that venom spilled into my relationship with my brother and sister.

Our family was not, as our surname suggests, "close." There was constant verbal abuse, emotional abuse, and physical beatings in our household. Parenting was at the end of a cane, with an extremely strict and prideful father ordering us to excel at school, behave ourselves in public, and make him look good—which meant to keep up the family facade.

Children were to be seen and not heard. My father said, "Do as I say, not as I do." As I matured, I understood why. Meanwhile, out of fear I was what my siblings called, the "goodie two-shoes" as I tried to please Dad and dodge bullets.

My mother had nothing to give, and I do not recall her ever hugging us, protecting us, or investing in us. However, I would have died for her. I was devoted to her and eagerly became her defender and rescuer until she destroyed my trust.

We were latchkey kids, and to this day, I cannot see a good reason why my parents had children. We did not bring them joy. Home life for me was filled with fears and tears. Frequently Dad said, "If you don't stop crying, I'll give you something to cry about," and then he gave me a savage belting.

As toddlers, my siblings and I were locked in the family car, outside a different drinking establishment every weekend. The late drives home each Friday, Saturday, and Sunday nights were often death-defying. My fear of us being killed in one of the car accidents was overwhelming. I survived on nervous energy. The traumas affected me for long periods, but nobody mentioned them. Life resumed as if they hadn't happened. I remember wishing my parents would get caught, punished, and locked away.

Drunkenness, anger, neglect, secrecy, and a public mask were just how we rolled. My parents were reckless and lost, and I am sad they never saw their damage to us nor looked for help.

As soon as my older sister turned ten, we three kids were left at home while my parents went on weekend drinking binges. What a relief. Although we fought constantly, we had some freedom—until we heard the car pull up outside. We ran for cover, anticipating a horror episode of violent fighting, hatred, and property damage. I felt powerless and believed one of my parents would die at the hands of the other, sooner or later. Relatives all lived too far away, so who could I turn to? And how could I betray my own parents?

I found comfort in being a "high achiever." At an early age, I did the family wash, cooked, cleaned, and was the obedient, reliable one. I managed straight A's for my entire school life and became high school captain. I am still shocked that nobody confronted me about the reality of my parents.

At eighteen, I was awarded a full academic scholarship and moved away to live on the university campus and attend teachers' college. Little did I know God had His hand on me. I can now see His many provisions through these messy years.

During college, I discovered that my father was not just the local drunk, but he was also the local marijuana grower and supplier to the hippy communes across the road from my high school. Such cruel hypocrisy. My mother had been having a long affair with my father's best friend. My older sister was evicted from nursing—for unruly behavior in the nurse's quarters and carelessness on the wards. She became pregnant and married a serial pedophile who had four wives, many children, and a serious drinking problem. He spent years in prison. My brother was given a dishonorable discharge from the Navy for being absent without leave for two years. He is still unable to commit to responsibility or a relationship.

Our parents did not care about any of us, did not ring up, offer help, or come to visit. I drove four hours to visit them, but nobody was home when I arrived. There was no food in the fridge or sheets on my bed. I felt total rejection. My brother and sister also lived as if I did not exist, making no contact. I finally stopped trying to fix my family, pay their bills, and make them happy—wishing we could all "straighten up and fly right." I graduated from college, moved to another state, and "divorced" my family. I did not see any of them for twenty years.

No one seemed to notice.

At college, it looked like I could become a respectable person of value and leave behind my chaotic upbringing. I was chosen to lead all women's sports on campus and won many leadership awards. In my final college year, I enjoyed the position of Senior Tutor, with responsibilities, benefits, and privileges.

I was highly motivated and worked hard, but I always felt that I didn't know how to grow up and be like others from good families. I was also damaged. The constant anxiety in my home had always driven me to consume food for comfort, which helped me stuff my emotions.

In an alcoholic home, the unspoken rules were: "Don't think. Don't feel. Don't tell."

By the time I was twenty, stress manifested itself as a rare condition that prevented me from being able to swallow. I had a major operation with limited success but enormous trauma.

I married the first man who took interest in me, the first man I met when I arrived at college. He too was a sportsman and a Senior Tutor. He was a heavy drinker, but I thought that was normal. We were the couple most likely to get married, have kids, and live happily ever after. Wrong. He was an alcoholic with a new girlfriend and serious liver damage at age twenty-seven.

After the divorce, I vowed I would never need or trust anyone. By then, my parents were divorced. My mother said I would land on my feet, and I was not to visit or bother her with my problems. If I ever had kids, I was not to bring them to her doorstep. I felt unwanted again. I was angry, became wild, and went traveling. I was accountable to no one, and that can be a very destructive place to be. I was convinced that nothing I did mattered to anyone, so there would be no consequences.

The rollercoaster sped up.

I was headed in a bad direction, making dumb decisions. I found it easy to make friends but couldn't keep them, because I couldn't trust them. I believed, if they really knew me, they wouldn't like me. I thought everyone except me and the Alcoholics Anonymous (AA) folks had their act together, and I would never quite cut it.

The week after my husband left me, I lost all control of the rollercoaster on a dirt road. At a high speed, my brand new car rolled four times. It was strangely exciting. I remember letting go of the steering wheel, expecting to die—hoping for "lights out, show's over." God had other plans. I walked backward away from that car wreck and wondered, *If there is a God, why has He just spared my life? Maybe I won't take life for granted anymore.*

I was invited to live with a loving family, who helped me get over both the accident and the marriage break-up. Truly another godsend. I later moved into my own apartment in a new town.

For the next few years, I was on a high, teaching precious kids of all ages. I was appointed to positions that others would kill for. But eventually, outside the work scene, I grew lonely and fell into bad company. A violent relationship with a drug user took me to a new depth. I believed I could rescue him, and he would change. Wrong again. Twice I contemplated suicide. I never took a drink, but food was my drug of choice. I became promiscuous, looking for love in all the wrong places. I became addicted to swimming and exercise. I spent a lot of time alone.

Twice I became seriously ill and had emergency surgery.

I wanted to get a grip on what happened during my childhood, so I attended AA meetings, then Adult Children of Alcoholics meetings. I understood the 12-step program.

I read all the self-help books I could get my hands on.

I understood the cycle of violence.

I understood the power of addiction.

I understood co-dependency and knew my own inappropriate survival skills.

I made a conscious decision that I would never have children, since I knew I would do no better than to repeat the destructive ways of my parents.

I devoted myself to teaching, because loving and teaching other people's children came easily to me. I could see what they needed academically and emotionally. I pretended they were my kids, and they loved me back. Nominated for the National Teaching Excellence Award, I was humbled by the gratitude and trust of my school communities.

However, I lived in fear of someone uncovering my shame, saying they knew my family, or asking why I was so hopeless at relationships, unmarried, with no kids.

By the year 2000, I was teaching in a classy city school, thoroughly enjoying my job. But I lacked something deeper. What was the point of my life? Shame, guilt, and regret had a powerful hold on me. I was living with a mask, just like before.

I needed rescue from the never-ending ride I was on.

By the grace of God, Steve Gaeth entered my life, the highest of my highs. Steve had been raised in a sweet, God-based family and enjoyed church life. He loved me. There was something extra special about him I couldn't explain. We were inseparable. I told him the whole ugly truth about my history. He didn't judge, criticize, or condemn me. I often asked to explore God and church, but I didn't know he had given up his faith.

Our romance was a fairy tale. I finally found a man who thought I was worthy of his time and company, but soon enough, my insecurities and lack of trust began to destroy our relationship. I owned my behaviors and told him I needed to go back to the 12-Step Alcoholics Anonymous program to gain sanity and self-control.

Steve said, "That twelfth step you talk about—that's Jesus."

I was confused. *What would Jesus have to do with it? Wasn't He just a storybook character for kids?*

A few days later, we saw a crowd of fully clothed people in the water at our beach. I laughed, and Steve said, "They are getting baptized."

They're what? My interest in God was stirred.

I continued being fractious. In April 2004, Steve said he was leaving.

I couldn't breathe. I had no reason to persist with a hollow, disappointing existence. What was the point of life without Steve? But I told him honestly that I would want to leave too if

I were in his shoes.

I took my swim gear and for the second time that day threw myself into the pool. Everything within me cried, "God, I need You. God, please help me. God, I can't do this." Lap after lap, I was desperate. I had nowhere to turn.

The next morning, by divine intervention, I walked to the local church and cried my heart out as I told the pastor my long and hopeless life-story. The pastor said, "You obviously believe in God, so get on your knees and say these words: *God, I need You. I am a sinner, and I apologize for all that I have done. I surrender my life to You. I believe in Jesus. I accept Him as Lord and Savior. In Jesus' name I pray, Amen.*"

I repeated that prayer and bowed humbly before this God Who I longed to know.

Then the pastor said, "Now, ring Steve and tell him you have just become a Christian."

"What does that mean?" I said. "I don't understand."

I felt like I had so much catching up to do. From that pivotal day, I have submitted to God. I learned who Jesus is and met with others to understand the Bible. Steve returned to living his life under God, the way he was raised. Finally I would learn the truth, the real point to life, and its eternal consequences. We attended church, got married, and made friends, who are still our friends today. God is real. Only He could have saved me from my self-destructive and pointless life.

The Bible tells us, "For *all*—that's every person except Jesus—have sinned and fall short of the glory of God." How amazing to be forgiven for everything and to know that when I die, I will stand joyfully before God. Jesus will welcome me into Heaven.

In 2009, I received news that my father had died. By the grace of God, Steve helped me be reconciled to my family. I chose to fully forgive my parents. I understood that they did not know any better, because they did not know God. I asked my mother and siblings to forgive me for the pain I had caused in their lives. They did not overly welcome me and were reluctant to hear about my experience with God, but their forgiveness set me free.

Nobody loved my parents into God's Kingdom. Nobody

showed them a different way. Sadly, they both died in their sin, and I don't expect to see them in Heaven. But I pray often for my brother and sister. The chains that pulled me down and held me guilty are gone. I have hope. And I want that for them and for you too.

The rollercoaster jolted back into motion in 2011. I handled it differently, because I trusted my God was at the helm. I claimed His healing power. A serious brain aneurysm almost took my life. There was talk of brain damage and a wheel chair.

Again, Steve was my anchor to God and sanity. He spent seventeen days in intensive care with me. He encouraged me at every stage. Due to his faith, he remained rock-solid, standing on God's faithfulness. I had two serious head surgeries and lost sight in one eye. Once I was home, I had serious nightmares. I spoke out the powerful scriptures that I had learned. There is power in the Word of God. I know it delivered me from mental torment, and when I said the name of Jesus, the devil fled.

It was then that Steve told me what happened the morning of the aneurysm. I had no recollection at all, but when I collapsed by the bed, I recited Psalm 23: "The Lord is my shepherd. I shall not want." I believe that is when I submitted, and God took over. After the whole Psalm, I started again, louder. "Yea, though I walk through the valley of the shadow of death, I will fear no evil, for thou art with me." All glory to God for His generous supply of miracles in my life. You see, I do not remember ever learning that scripture from start to finish. I was unconscious for two-and-a-half hours before I was examined by a neurosurgeon who exclaimed, "This is highly unusual. The bleeding has stopped, and I can't explain that."

God trusted me to come through that near-death experience by praising Him in the worst of circumstances and believing what He says in the Bible. My character was reshaped through tough times like this. Today I live by faith in Jesus Christ. Maybe He saved me so you could hear my story.

Fifteen years into my relationship with God, I still love being in His will, because my will was so dangerous and chaotic. There is power in what Jesus offers. And I am grateful every day. Being in marriage under covenant with God, to a man who fears and loves God, while standing on the biblical truths, is a contented place to be. I rejoice in knowing I stand before mankind as a transformed person. God is real, and He is good. Only He holds the power to transform us.

Without God, I was stiff-necked and hard-hearted. But more than that, I was ignorant. Ignorance would not have gotten me a free pass into Heaven. There are no valid excuses for rejecting Jesus Christ.

I want to praise God for picking up the pieces, healing my confusion, regret, bitterness, disillusionment, and using His superglue to put me back together. He's shown me that He is more interested in my character than in my comfort. God has given my life beauty I don't deserve, in exchange for the pile of ashes I created.

He has numbered my days, and He orders my steps. I no longer have white knuckles from the fear of losing my grip and catapulting off the rails. I am convinced that we were created by God for relationship with Him. He has a unique purpose for each of us to live out. If He can save a wretch like me, He will do it for anyone who asks. Thank you for sharing the ride.

Mandy Gaeth, a teacher, grew up along the beautiful sunny beaches of Queensland in Australia, and recently moved to the United States with her husband, Steve, who is the one who began to tell her about the goodness of God. She eagerly surrendered her life to God at age 45, and through that divine relationship, God continues to bring her the joy and hope that she never knew while growing up.

Thoughts to Ponder
from Rollercoaster

1. We are restored by God.

2. There is no partiality or condemnation in Christ.

3. God can level out our ups and downs.

What rollercoaster are you on right now?

The path of the righteous is level;
you, the Upright One, make the way
of the righteous smooth. — Isaiah 26:7

Calling on God
by Tovar Holmes

Standing next to my bed with my hands firmly gripping the sheet, I flailed my arms up with the sheet billowing out, spanning the width and length of the bed. My arms now descending to my sides without warning, the room began to spin. The dresser drawers, the windows, the curtains, the pictures on the walls, and the walls themselves swirled around me. With my feet beginning to slip out from under me, I held on to the sheet for balance. When that didn't work, I quickly grabbed the side of the bed. I waited for the room to stop spinning. After what seemed like an eternity, I no longer felt like I was falling.

I checked the room again. It was still, and I climbed onto the bed. "Lord, please don't. Don't do this!" In spite of my pleas, after a trip to the doctor and a few tests, the warning signs were confirmed: I was pregnant. Fear, anxiety, and insecurity set in like a deer being stalked by a lion. I wanted to hide and pretend this predicament was not mine. Running away as fast as I could seemed like a good idea.

I don't know how I'm going to do this, and furthermore, I don't want to do this.

Why wouldn't I be happy? I was married with two children who would love a little brother or sister, right? Those are the sentiments to be shared with someone who has a health history that is unscathed—not to someone who lay in the hospital bed the year before, praying to God to save her life. Not to someone who was told, before she left the hospital, not to have any more children. Not to someone who was two weeks away from a scheduled tubal ligation. Not to someone like me.

The year before, as I lay in the hospital bed, uncertain of whether I would live, the doctor did all he could. But he could not guarantee my life. He encouraged me to read my Bible even though I questioned whether he was a Christian. He wanted me to grab hold of anything I could believe in. He quietly said, as though he was thinking out loud, "If you make it through the night, you will be okay. We need you to make it through the night." He would do the medicine part, but the rest was up to God.

The word God gave me at that time was 2 Timothy 1:7: "For the Spirit God gave us does not make us timid, but gives us power, love and self-discipline." Morning came, and the doctor was the first to rush in. He ordered the nurses to remove the IVs. I could see he was relieved. I knew God as my Healer. I left that hospital without fear, with the love of God and a very sound mind. And one stipulation: *Don't have any more children!*

But here I was, a year later, being told I was pregnant. The doctor who confirmed my pregnancy looked at the medications I had been taking. She reviewed my medical history, which revealed that I had been diagnosed and hospitalized with pulmonary emboli. We both stood there, about the same age. I was thirty-three, but we obviously stood in very different positions.

She had a panicked look. "It says your baby could have complications, possible deformities, and this pregnancy could be life threatening for both of you. You may want to consider an abortion."

"I may want to do what?" The words swirled around me like I was caught in the eye of a tornado. I felt like debris was flying all around me, and I couldn't see clearly. "I can't do that."

She inquired and probed me with a puzzled look.

All I could respond with was the truth. "My faith and my relationship with God won't allow me to do that."

I can't remember every detail of what happened next. I remember that she shook her head as if to dismiss my foolishness. I somehow received a referral for a high-risk doctor. How I got home that day and made it through the next few days is a blur to me.

I wasn't sure what to do next, except I knew I had to go to God. I promised God I would not have an abortion. It was a promise made long ago, but it was still a promise. Was I being tested? In my time with God, I prayed for Him to give me a word I could hold on to, a scripture I could believe as I went through this uncertain journey. I was led to Jeremiah 33:3: "Call to me and I will answer you and tell you great and unsearchable things you do not know." I needed something great and mighty, something I had never known or seen before. My very life and my baby's life depended on it. I had to find some faith for both of us—something I had never experienced before. I had to believe what could not be explained. I had to believe.

There was no guarantee I would live through this and no guarantee for my baby. I was desperate for an answer, desperate for comfort, and desperate for something I could believe and hold on to. I could not get answers from doctors. People dismissed me as foolish, just as the doctor already had. In addition to all that, I had just moved to Houston, and I didn't know anyone. I joined a church, but once again, relationships had not yet been formed. I was alone.

Life and the pregnancy continued. I was exhausted all the time, and I began to avoid people and their calls. Socialization was too much effort. I knew there were some who meant well, but I didn't want to talk. The doctors meant well, but they were limited to medical advice, medications, referrals, and occasional words of encouragement, though carefully arranged to not give me false hope.

My daily scripture readings and time with God faded. I joined a new Bible study. However, the time conflicted with my doctor appointments. It was the only day my high-risk ob-gyn was available. I asked my new church members for prayer, and I left the Bible study. I had to drive to the medical center on those Mondays, and appointments were tiring because they took the whole day. I will forever be grateful for one thing about my high-risk ob-gyn.

When I first arrived at her office, the young woman greeted me with a caring yet comfortable confidence. She was different from the first doctor. In her office, she shared all my options in a matter-of-fact way. She relayed what the pregnancy might or might not involve regarding treatment. She shared statistics and gave me resources to look up about people in similar conditions. She also shared the option of abortion. When I replied with my choice to proceed with the pregnancy, there were no strange or panicked looks, coaxing, additional heeding of medical mishaps or warnings. She simply replied with, "Okay, and this is what we will do next." She was on my side, on a mission to deliver a healthy baby and keep its mother alive and well. I knew it, and the Holy Spirit comforted me with it. She was heaven-sent.

I continued to hold on to the Jeremiah 33:3 verse, and I called on God again and again, reminding Him of His promise to me. I tried to sleep away most of my waking moments. All I could rehearse in my mind and say out loud was, "Call to me and I will answer and tell you great and unsearchable things you have not known." When I was alone, I screamed the words out loud. At night, I quietly recited them as tears ran down my face and wet my pillow. I needed God—He was all I had.

I continued to struggle with people, my husband included, and I became more and more withdrawn. I slept any chance I could get. My older boys, who were now six and eight, were such good kids. But I was not the mom I used to be. Often I didn't want to join them on fun outings. Playing with them took too much effort. The truth was, I didn't want to join anyone in anything. Occasionally I came out of my cocoon when I recognized I *had* to, usually at my husband's insistence. Although I am introverted by nature, he knew this was not me, and he insisted that I at least ask the doctor why I was sleeping so much. I did, and she listened and continued with our visit. After getting off the subject and back onto the subject, she said, "I'm concerned that you may be depressed."

Really, me depressed? But I just accepted it, took the pills, and continued. I didn't consider what that really meant. Little did I know that it was the beginning of bigger depression battles ahead.

Deep down, I didn't want to hear what other people thought. I didn't want their advice or their pity. I didn't want to pretend around them either. Everything was not all right, and I didn't want to act like it was. I was in a battle for my life, and my strength was being zapped daily. Since I had been told the year before not to have any more children, I had put the idea to rest and started a new business, which was going well. I was making plans. I was always looking forward to the next thing, and the future was what I lived for. Looking back, I can see that my thoughts and so much of my life was askew.

I felt like I knew what friends, family, and the doctors also knew—or maybe they didn't. I knew they could not do what God could do. Not one of them, and not all of them together.

Only He could sustain my baby's life and my life. Only He could equip me and my family for the challenges if I suffered a stroke. Only He could enable me to be a parent to a baby with disabilities. Only He could take care of my family if one or both of us perished. Only He could make us whole if we lived. Only God could show me something great and unsearchable if I called on Him. And I called on Him. I cried, and I pleaded. And I called on Him some more. I knew He was real, and I was real to Him. Although I was alone in this world, I would not let God leave me alone too.

The baby was growing just fine, and no major complications arose, but I was on medications. The shots were the worst. I had to give myself injections of blood thinners in the last three months of my pregnancy. I hated them, and my hands trembled most of the time, two to three times a day, whenever I had to inject myself. I remember the frustration and the pain of the needles piercing my belly. Once, with tears pouring down my face, I threw the entire syringe with the medication contents across the bathroom. I hated what I was going through.

I had dreams that taunted and sometimes haunted me. I felt Satan was putting every doubt possible into my mind. I felt the lack of hope of those around me.

One night, I dreamed that I was leaning down, reaching into the stroller as my baby began to cry. As my eyes fell on the baby, his eyes were abnormal, his eyelids droopy. In that moment, I became aware that my husband had left me because he did not want anything to do with either one of us. When I awakened, I knew this was only a dream, but doubt still lurked in the back of my mind. My husband never threatened to leave me. And I really had no evidence to support any abnormalities in my baby. We didn't have as many ultrasounds as I had experienced in my other pregnancies. The doctor felt no need, and my decision was made. I didn't want to know anything either, at least not yet. I already had enough to deal with, and my nightmares certainly didn't help.

Trayse was born on October 4, 2002, at 12:43 p.m. by cesarean section. Out came a screaming baby and a beautiful one indeed. When the doctor handed him to me, swaddled in a blanket, I looked at my baby's face. All I could see were two big, bright, round, and yes, perfect eyes.

God saw my nightmare, and He knew my fears. He reassured me right away. *I am bigger than any attack you received from Satan. And yes, I can do what doctors can't. I am your Healer, the giver of life. Your life, your baby's, your husband, and your children are in My hands. I am here. I Am that I Am. When you called to Me, Tovar, I heard you, and now you have My answer. I am God, and I have shown you things, great, mighty, and unsearchable, miraculous things you have never known.*

God went on to heal Trayse and me in life. I don't know why God chose to spare my life twice or why He chose to heal me and my son the way He did. Some people say it is because God has something for me to do. I believe He has something for all of us to do, even if He calls us home to be with Him. But I did ask Him, "Why all this, God? Why did You let me go through this?" He was gracious to grant me an answer. I am fully aware that God owes us no explanations. Just a few verses after Jeremiah 33:3, there is much suffering that falls on the people of Judah and Israel. Verse six says, "Nevertheless, I will bring health and healing to it; I will heal my people and will let them enjoy abundant peace and security." And that is what God did for me as well.

I felt God impress upon me, *I didn't send you this baby to hurt you, hinder you, or harm you. I sent you this baby to help you.* And He did.

I needed to learn how to let go and let God be God. So I learned to slow down. I stopped living for the next thing. I realized there is no future if you don't invest time in the present. I learned how to really enjoy my children, not just care for them or teach them, but to relax and love them.

Trayse challenged me again and again. He would not sleep well, he was super busy, and he always said or did something unexpected, which usually left me embarrassed in front of others. I learned to let go of judgment. I had been on the other side of it too often. I walked away from my business and invested time in caring for Trayse, my older boys, my husband, and even myself. I also learned how to accept help, how to ask for it, and most importantly, how to offer it.

God doesn't intend for us to be alone, and usually the times when we *want* to be alone are when we least *need* to be alone.

People are in our lives for a reason. We shouldn't push everyone away when we have problems.

I also had to let go of control. I couldn't control most things in life. I spent most of my time confused about what I could control. I had to let go and trust God. I learned to smile and have fun again. It felt like God was saying, "You can rest in Me and you don't have to do everything yourself. I am here. I am here *with you* and all you have to do is call Me."

Tovar Holmes has been married for 25 years with three amazing sons and her very first granddaughter. She is involved in ministry and teaches new believers at her home church. Tovar gives thanks to God for being blessed by our Lord and Savior with a gift of writing. A collection of her poems can be found in a published anthology Conversing through Poetry. *Tovar will write almost anything she can to encourage others in their walk with God. And finally, Trayse is currently in high school, plays football, and most of all, is healthy.*

Thoughts to Ponder

from Calling on God

1. God is our healer.

2. We must be willing to have faith in God, because He is faithful.

3. God hears our prayers and answers according to His will.

> **When was the last time you called on God?**

Call to me and I will answer you and tell you great and unsearchable things you do not know. — Jeremiah 33:3

Heart of Stone
by Helene Terry

I'll never forget the taste of charcoal. When I learned of my husband's affair, I was twenty-three years old, bright, and talented. Unfortunately, I lost my grip on seeing a positive future. In an afternoon of feeling desolate, with no thought of a rewarding future, I tried to check out with an overdose of prescription drugs, chased with alcohol. As a last desperate plea, I called my husband to say goodbye, and he followed up by having emergency services dispatched. As a result, my life was saved in the ER as they pumped out the lethal contents from my stomach and applied the activated charcoal to reduce the absorption.

How did an outgoing, cute, high school girl with the Senior Superlative of "Best Personality" have all her dreams taken away by trusting in the wrong mate? Why was there no spiritual depth when I had been raised so faithfully in a good church?

I wish I could say I addressed these issues, but after my father died, I placed *myself* in charge of my life. Until he was killed in a plane crash at the age of forty-nine, my dad had been my main spiritual influencer. He was taking his Sunday school class for rides when the accident happened. Four lives were lost that day, while many spectators from the group watched in horror.

My mother was non-nurturing and by this time had little influence on my life. When I was a young child, she insisted we call her Mother. We could not call her mommy or mama, because she did not like those names. She exuded little warmth, which also factored into my chubbiness as a child. Though I slimmed down and turned heads as an attractive twenty-three-year-old, the low self-esteem demon seemed comfortably lodged inside.

Therefore, I didn't seek help navigating through the abandonment, suicide attempt, and divorce. My brilliant remedy was to guard my heart in future relationships. Rather than let anyone have the upper hand with my emotions, I would be the *heartbreaker*. I definitely followed the motto of "work hard, play hard." I was dedicated to both.

For my twenty-fifth birthday party, my cake was decorated with the words, "Drugs, Sex, and Rock & Roll," which should tell you something about the life I was living. Not only did I know the bars in Nashville, but I also knew the after-bars. On weekdays, I kept my career flowing smoothly and was always a dependable worker. The weekends were another story. One reason I moved from Nashville to Dallas in 1982 was to change my friends and party scenes. Funny how my "wild ways" moved with me. It really wasn't due to anyone else's "bad influence."

When I found myself pregnant and unmarried at the age of twenty-seven, I never took my eyes off the abortion clinic on Fairmont Avenue in Dallas. I did not tell the father of the baby, my girlfriends, my family, or anyone else. *I* took care of it and had very few tears, further demonstrating my internal hardness.

How can a girl who went to a Bible-believing church three times a week for seventeen years have such a heart of stone? In my youth, I won Bible drills. I attended summer church camp so many times, the counselors were confused as to which was my home church. While all of this was good, I never had a personal relationship with God—thus the emptiness. I remember "the prayer" for salvation at age eight, but my dad said it for me and then checked it off *his* list.

I did not personally engage in a relationship with God. To make things more confusing, we looked like a normal suburban "good family." I was raised by both parents, and we enjoyed a comfortable lifestyle due to my father's successful business. My mother worked part-time in seasonal tax work. She was certainly there for me physically, but never emotionally. How did I reach this age looking normal on the outside, and yet I was such a wreck on the inside?

The train wreck continued. Sex was my language of love, and I had my share of boyfriends who spoke the same language. Since my heart was encased in granite, my conscience was not bothered. I buried it all and looked like a happy, carefree, laughing young woman who had a career, friends, and dates. I was prosperous and had no real worries in life.

This continued into my thirties—until I met the most gorgeous man and fell in love. We were party people, yet true to

110

each other. After two years of dating, he proposed. We had a wedding and married to "live happily ever after," which in our case was about one month. When we learned that we were pregnant, I stopped my partying, and he increased his.

One weekend when he disappeared, I was looking for him and somehow found myself talking to a counselor, who had the audacity to talk about my mental state. My problem was *him*, and only that. Did she not see this as clearly as I did?

However, despite the turmoil, on November 19, 1989, my precious baby girl was born. That was when I really began to understand love. At the same time, I acknowledged another "aha" moment. *If I absolutely adore her, why didn't my parents adore me?* Everything she did was celebrated, which made me see how "uncelebrated" I was to my family.

I was the baby of the family, with a sister and brother a few years older than me. Maybe my mother was simply tired by the time I came along. I had been well-provided for, physically, yet I lived in an emotional desert. We didn't argue or fight. We also didn't kiss or hug one another. We merely existed, which left emotional damage that later "qualified" me for intensive therapy.

No wonder my emotional radar was so off. At this point, my husband centered his priorities around bars and alcohol. As a result, I decided to search high and low for a book titled "How to Successfully Live with an Alcoholic." I could not find such a book, although I did find Alcoholics Anonymous. I was concerned about the damage an alcoholic home would have on my daughter. I realized I needed to take her to church so she would learn a better way. This was one of my more rational ideas.

When I was a kid, I had a lapel pin that I wore at church. Each year that I did not miss a Sunday, a bar was added to the pin. When we moved, I had seven bars, which represented an enormous amount of teaching, as well as an additional ten years of sermons and exposure to spiritual things. However, I was hardened, and like Pavlov's dog was trained to salivate with the ringing of a bell, when I heard church lingo and certain phrases, my mind turned off and the daydreaming began.

The good news is that my baby girl was in the church

nursery, dolled up with ruffles and bows, and I was in the congregation, listening to the songs and the message. This time was different. I wasn't daydreaming, and I truly heard words of wisdom. I received Christ as my Savior, and started trusting in His guidance rather than my own. My heart of stone softened, and I finally realized that God loved me unconditionally. All have sinned and need forgiveness, and God sent His Son, Jesus, to die for everyone's sin, including mine.

My distorted thoughts had led me down the wrong paths, and it was time to give up and follow Him. John 15:5 says, "Apart from me you can do nothing." My way had not worked out, so I needed a personal relationship with Jesus so He could be the feeder vine in my life, bringing a harvest of spiritual fruit.

My husband did not follow my new lifestyle, and though I tried to save the marriage, he wanted a divorce. Soon after, I joined a Christian intensive therapy group to deal with my raging anger and sadness. Becoming a Christian was "step one" to becoming more like Jesus.

I wanted to learn my pitfalls, trust in God, and avoid my former destructive paths. When attending the outpatient program, I could not believe I was on par with other members of the group, who had so many bizarre problems. For a month, we each worked through our issues, meeting five nights a week for three hours. When my "stuff" started surfacing, I felt truly qualified to be part of the group.

The non-nurturing and non-emotional household from my "good" home had created intensive damage, and while many of my group members also suffered worse physical damage, we were each broken in our own way. Obviously, I needed to participate so I could find healing. Low self-esteem has no economic or life-condition barriers. Both wealthy and poverty-stricken people can suffer greatly from this issue, and it takes time to realize how worthy we are to God, ourselves, and others.

This turning point helped me understand my need so I could take steps to stop my destructive behavior. My therapist guided me to allow my daughter to maintain a relationship with my in-laws, though her father was not involved in her life. Over the years, I firmly believe their nurturing ways and constant, loving involvement in my daughter's life helped her become a self-confident young lady who knows she is loved. Because of the anger I had for my ex-husband, I almost threw away that relationship. Without the wise counsel of a godly therapist, I could have negatively changed the trajectory of my daughter's life, as well as my own.

I believe therapy is important, because we play negative tapes over and over in our minds, which keeps us going in circles. Satan loves these tapes, and many times he is at the mixer board, pushing all the levels up to keep us stuck. Therefore, we must find others to help change our tapes. Going it alone is a great way to remain on the same destructive path. Someone once said that self-help is no help. If we are blind to our issues, how can we see the way to a new path?

Several years later, I wanted to serve in my church's Crisis Pregnancy Center. Because I had an abortion, they wisely required my attendance at their Abortion Recovery program. Half of that program was needed for me to thaw out the numbed and stuffed feelings about my abortion. For the last half, I was able to start processing my feelings.

After I completed the program, they asked me to serve as an observer, which I did twice. God knew what He was doing, because it was not until I completed the third session that I could publicly admit I had taken the life of my baby boy, who is now skipping in Heaven with Jesus. One day, I will be reunited with him and witness his sweet self. I am only able to have these positive thoughts because of the work I did in the recovery program.

The changes in my life have taken purposeful dedication and have not happened overnight. After one area has been addressed, capacity is opened to address another area.

I continue to be a work in progress, and I will be for the rest of my life. Even as recently as 2011, much to my surprise, I reunited with my first husband and started a "missionary dating" relationship. You might know what that is. The guy isn't yet a Christian, but through your wonderful influence you expect him to surrender to God's ways. If any of you are involved in that, run for the hills. When guys are infatuated with a woman, they will do and say anything to snag her. Once the prize is secured, they will usually revert to their old ways. That's what happened to me.

While dating, my ex had great church attendance and was involved with the men's ministry. In the end, he married me while still being married. That qualified us for an annulment and took me to a very dark place. It was the first time I had ever experienced being *angry* at God.

I had prayed for God's guidance in the relationship, so how did I end up in yet another mess? I soon learned the simple answer. Though I prayed, I was not in His Word to hear His guidance. This is when I experienced a major paradigm shift of truly seeking God through His Word, prayer, and community. There are no shortcuts in this process. There are no magic pills. By 2013, I found a great church body and experienced my true community of believers, my new adopted family.

Now, my goal is to assist others in avoiding the same pain I experienced. I want to help them find an exit door to the destructive path they are traveling.

Life still presents challenges for me. Raising my daughter alone wasn't easy. Her father gave up all his legal rights to her and never contributed financially. At the same time, I have been blessed beyond measure and have found forgiveness for him—a miracle in itself. My sweet baby girl is now a wife and mother, and the "sins of the father" have been squelched. In fact, she now leads others out of human trafficking. One night, I was visiting a safe home for teenage girls, where she was the co-director. She was comforting a girl by singing one of the spiritual songs I had sung to her as a baby.

What about all the "junk" of our past? God is ready and able to redeem the years. One of my favorite verses is Joel 2:25: "I will repay you for the years the locusts have eaten." When I heard my daughter singing that song, I knew He had restored many of my lost years, and He will do the same for you.

Through that awful-tasting charcoal, God saved me at the age of twenty-three, because He has always had a purpose in my life and the life of my daughter. He created diamonds from the stones around my heart. If he can use my "junk," He can do the same for you. This only happened when I trusted in Him and got out of His way. The incredible science lesson I learned is that diamonds are created when charcoal is subjected to extreme pressure.

Are you ready for God to make diamonds out of your life? Give your heart to Him, and watch as He crafts beautiful gems that will sparkle when you reflect His light.

Helene Terry *serves on the Women's Ministry team at Reunion Church, is a board member of Exodus Ministries, and also supports Redeemed Women in Dallas. Her profession as a residential Kitchen Designer began over thirty years in Knoxville, Tennessee, and her award-winning work has been published in* This Old House, LUXE, Kitchen and Bath Business, NKBA Profile, D-Home, Design Guide, Texas Home and Living, Dallas Style, and Great American Kitchens *magazines. She is a member of Fellowship of Professional Women of Dallas, past board member of ASID Dallas Design Community, past president and board chairman of the Dallas Executives Association and former member of the Kitchen Advisory Committee at The Art Institute of Dallas. Reach her at* **HelenesLuxuryKitchens@gmail.com.**

Thoughts to Ponder
from Heart of Stone

1. The hardest of hearts can be softened by God.

2. The Word of God will always provide direction.

3. We are a work in progress until the day we die.

Where does your heart need to soften?

I will give you a new heart and put a new spirit in you;
I will remove from you your heart of stone and give you
a heart of flesh. — Ezekiel 36:26

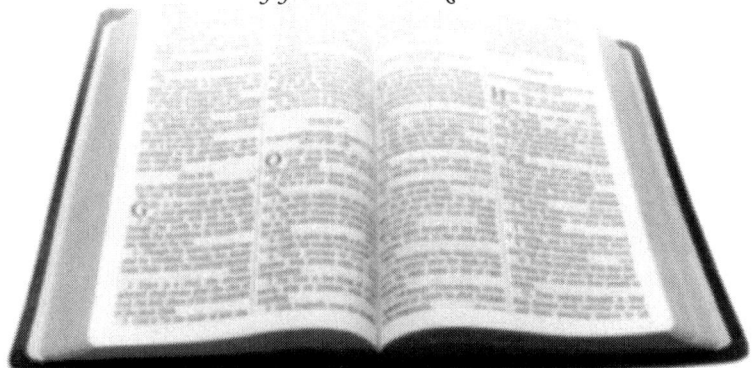

From Depression to Joy
by Patty Mason

Standing onstage in Dallas, before an audience of thousands, I was being recognized for one of the highest levels of achievement in the company. My heart sank. Surrounded by joyful celebration, I thought, *Is this all there is?* In the loud music and thunderous applause, I thought, *Is this what I shipped my children off to a babysitter for? Is this what I did the changing of the guard with my husband for?* Suddenly, everything I had poured myself into that year felt worthless. In the middle of what should have been a magnificent moment, I fell from a momentary high to a miserable point of confusion. I cried on the plane all the way home.

In the days following the conference, I turned my back on everything and everyone I thought would bring me happiness. I became critical of everything my husband and children did or didn't do. The career I had once loved became pointless. I wandered through each day like a blind beggar, not knowing what I was begging for. I couldn't overcome the feelings of sadness and worthlessness. Each day became increasingly harder—every minute increasingly darker.

I was thirty-five years old and had everything this world deemed valid. I had a husband who loved me, three beautiful children, a nice home, and a successful career. I had achieved everything I set out to accomplish. Yet I was miserable. I had everything I had dreamed of, but nothing brought me happiness and fulfillment.

What should have been my greatest journey toward satisfaction turned out to be my worst nightmare. Nothing made me happy. Nothing made me whole. Nothing gave me the sense of life, love, and purpose I was searching for. Trying to find myself, I had lost myself. I didn't have a clue where to turn.

I didn't want to admit that I was falling apart emotionally and spiritually. Admitting my inner being was a mess meant failure. Outwardly I appeared to have it all, so how could I tell others I was miserable? I believed the lie that I had to be great, self-reliant, and perfect. I couldn't look like I had a great life and then say, "I'm not okay." So I kept everything locked inside and pretended. Every day, I worked hard at wearing the mask, trying to convince others that nothing was wrong, but inwardly, I was dying.

I did my best to fix myself—to find answers, to get better, to stop feeling the way I did. But nothing helped. I didn't want to admit that I couldn't help myself, that I needed to look beyond myself to find relief. What would others think? Would they judge me, criticize me, and condemn me for feeling this way? They might stop loving me, or stop being my friends.

Until this point, no one, not even my husband, knew about the pain I was going through. So when I found courage to talk about the depression, no one judged, criticized, or condemned me. They just didn't believe me.

Feeling cheated and betrayed, I began to push away the people I loved. During the depression, I never felt lonelier. Even my sweet husband didn't get it. Almost every night, I tried to tell him something was wrong. Each time, he said, "Oh, you'll get over it." My husband loved me. I knew that, but he didn't understand what I was going through.

After exhausting all efforts to find help through family and friends, I turned to the medical profession. With phonebook in hand, I thought, *If I could get some pills, I'll be fine.* I had a get-fixed-quick mentality and figured a simple prescription would do the trick. So I went down the list, calling doctor after doctor, only to hear responses like, "I'm sorry, we don't take your insurance," or "We don't handle that kind of depression."

In less than an hour, I finished the entire list of professional doctors. When I dialed the last number, a kind woman answered and listened patiently to my heartfelt plea, only to tell me, "I'm sorry, but we can't help you." As I hung up the phone, I thought, *No one can help me. I'm utterly alone. This is never going to end.* At that moment, the darkness became darker, and suicidal thoughts entered my mind.

When I realized I was completely alone in my struggle, hopelessness turned to desperation. I had to do something to end the suffering—not only for myself but also for my family. I knew committing suicide was wrong, and my actions would hurt my family tremendously. However, the darkness was so thick

118

and heavy, I didn't see another answer. Death seemed to be the only way out, and I convinced myself that everyone would be better off without me.

In the days that followed, I found myself doing something I rarely did—I prayed. As a child, my exposure to God and church was punitive. When my parents took me to church, I saw a man standing at the front, calling all of us sinners. I didn't understand the allegation, so his accusations only made me mad. Church intimidated me. From my perspective, church was a place of burdensome rules and mechanical rituals. So when I became old enough to make my own decisions, I stopped going.

Praying to a God I didn't know felt foreign, but I didn't know what else to do. I was desperate to end the pain, but I didn't pray for God's help, mercy, or healing. Nor did I call on Him for answers. Instead, I asked Him to take my life. Every morning, I prayed for the insanity to end. Every night, I prayed to never wake up.

The most crucial point came on December 12, 1996. I couldn't go on, not even one more day. When I awoke that morning, I felt angry. I lay in bed, staring at the ceiling, and thought, *Why won't You let me die?*

Reluctantly, I got up and stepped into the shower. Hot tears of frustration poured from my eyes. Naked, drenched, and ashamed, I felt like I had been ground into the ashes from which I came. There was nothing left. I had reached the end of myself. And through the sobs, I talked to God. "I have nowhere else to go but You," I said. "You have to do something. No one can help me. Only You can help me! Please, help me."

This time, I didn't ask God to end my life. I asked Him for much more. I asked for a miracle. This was a desperate make-it-or-break-it moment. If God didn't do something that day, I feared I would. My plea was not an ultimatum. I wasn't bargaining with God. I had hit rock bottom. I had nowhere else to go.

Through the sobs, I heard what sounded like a faint voice, saying, *Go to MOPS* (Mothers of Preschoolers). I moaned. I didn't want to be around people. I didn't want to pretend that everything was fine. As my emotions were persuading me to stay home, I heard the voice again. *Go to MOPS.*

With my son in tow, I arrived at MOPS and immediately put on the mask that said I was doing well. I didn't want the ladies to know about my emotional turmoil, and I certainly didn't want them to know about my suicidal thoughts.

Toward the latter part of the meeting, the speaker came forward and stood behind the podium. She shared what it's like to lack joy and have no real purpose in life. She didn't specifically talk about depression, but what she was saying fell in line with what I was feeling. The crux of her message was about finding joy and purpose in life, and the only way to find pure joy was through Jesus Christ.

As she stepped from the platform and headed toward the back of the room, I got up without thinking and followed her. She looked at me and smiled warmly. I don't remember how our conversation started. Before I knew it, I found myself dumping my life at her feet. Without warning, an emotional dam broke, and I rambled and sobbed uncontrollably.

I couldn't control what was happening. I couldn't stop crying. I couldn't stop talking—not even when I realized every woman in the room had turned to stare at us. By that point, I didn't care who knew or what they thought. I needed help, and this woman seemed to have the answer.

She listened quietly for several minutes. Then, without saying a word, she touched my left arm, and when she did, the hysterics stopped. My crying and run-on sentences stopped. The nausea in the pit of my stomach vanished. The dark cloud that had been my constant companion disappeared. The heaviness lifted. All the darkness that had consumed my life was gone. My spirit and soul felt light, like they had taken on wings and could fly around the room. For the first time, I felt free.

I was stunned and completely amazed. I stood and stared at her, frozen by what had taken place. I had no idea if she knew or understood what had happened, because she still hadn't said a word. Yet there was something about her that I had never known before. As I looked into her eyes, I saw great love and tender compassion.

When I walked away, I tried to comprehend the experience. I knew this woman didn't possess the power to heal me, but God did. Suddenly, peace had washed over me. There was no other explanation. It was a miracle. Even though I didn't fully understand what had happened, I was convinced that the power I felt rush through me was God answering my desperate plea for help.

The next week, I was filled with joy. Instantly, my life rose from the darkness and burst with delight. Laughter and joy filled my heart, and a sense of pleasure overtook my soul. A huge weight came off me. I was undeniably transformed and could not stop thinking about Jesus.

Although I was set free from the symptoms of depression, God had more in mind than I could ever imagine. It wasn't enough for me to find His joy and peace. He wanted me to find Him. He wanted me to know more than the goodness of His mercy and compassion. He wanted me to know His intimate love through a personal relationship.

On December 18, 1996, at four o'clock that afternoon, my children had hair appointments at a local salon. As I waited for them, I noticed a poster advertising a Christmas play at a local church. *I have to go*, I thought. The program was at seven o'clock. By the time my children's haircuts were finished, it was almost five o'clock. Quickly, I put them in the car and drove to the church to see if tickets were still available. Since it was late in the afternoon, only the church secretary was in the office.

"Do you have any tickets left for tonight's performance?"

"No, I'm sorry," she said. "We're all sold out."

Heartbroken, I thanked her and turned to leave. But before I could step over the threshold, she said, "But come anyway. Come early, and we'll find you a seat." Overjoyed, I thanked her and said I would.

That night, the church was packed. Even with no tickets, the usher politely helped us find seats. The program was broken into four unique performances. In the final act, the church reenacted the birth of Jesus. As a child, I had seen the reenactment several times on television. Yet none of it touched me the way this one did. It was like I was seeing the birth of Jesus for the first time.

When the program finished, the pastor took the stage and talked about God's grace, Jesus' redemptive love, and how to find salvation through Jesus alone. I had no idea what he was talking about. All I knew was that I needed Jesus. Without hesitation, I responded, echoing the pastor's words as heavy tears streaked my face. Because of what Jesus had done for me, I opened my heart to Him.

God wanted to set me free from the suffering. However, He had a different way of ending it. I thought the only way out was death, but God had other plans. When I saw devastation, God saw promise. When I saw hopelessness, God saw a way to bring me near. The depression felt to me like the end, but to God, the depression was just the beginning of a whole new life with Him.

Patty Mason, wife, mother, grandmother, author, mentor, and founder of Liberty in Christ Ministries, has encouraged millions with God's Word through Light Source and as the host of Joyful Living Radio. She has appeared on American Family Radio, Moody Radio, and The 700 Club. She has written several books and Bible studies, including Finally Free: Breaking the Bonds of Depression Without Drugs, Experiencing Joy: Strategies for Living a Joy Filled Life, *and* The Power of Hope. *To learn more about Patty, her books, or Liberty in Christ Ministries, visit **LibertyinChristMinistries.com.***

Thoughts to Ponder
from From Depression to Joy

1. When a situation appears hopeless, God makes a way.

2. No matter how successful we become, the world cannot determine our worth or satisfy us.

3. Pure joy is only found through Jesus Christ.

Where have you looked to find happiness and satisfaction in life?

Then they cried to the Lord in their trouble, and he saved them from their distress. He sent out his word and healed them; he rescued them from the grave. — Psalm 107:19–20

Tearing Down the Walls

by Alison Vorlicky

My name is Alison Vorlicky, and I have been sober from the world for fourteen years. I know this probably sounds funny, like I am standing up at an Alcoholics Anonymous meeting, stating my name and how long I have been sober from alcohol, but it is my reality.

Fourteen years ago, I was in a dark and lonely place, where drugs were my mechanism for coping with the deep pains of my soul. After begging and pleading with an unknown God to rescue me from the treacherous waters that were drowning me, I surrendered my life to the Lord. He quickly grabbed hold of me and brought me back to dry land, breathing life into my desolate soul. From that moment on, I have been on a healing journey with the Lord, and I am overcoming the weight of the world.

What caused my deep night of the soul? Let's go back to the beginning.

I was born and raised in New York and attended college at Ohio State University. I now live in Dallas, Texas, with a New York accent, a little bit of hillbilly, and a whole lot of y'alls. So when I speak, it might be confusing. Despite the confusion, I know Who I belong to.

I grew up in a dysfunctional Jewish family, with a father who had an abusive, heated temper. He abused my mother, and sometimes that abuse was directed toward my sister, brother, and me. At the age of six, I was sexually molested by a close family friend. After that, I had vivid dreams of being abducted and raped. As the years passed, those dreams turned into nightmares of my father raping me. The pain and anguish through those haunting dreams led me to attempt suicide.

After graduating from high school, I went to Ohio State, where my rebellious days began. I was free from all control, abuse, and triggers. Sex, drugs, and alcohol became my way of coping with life. I looked for love and acceptance in all the wrong places. The more sex I had, the more I numbed the disgust I had when looking in the mirror.

In 2003, my life took a dramatic turn for the better. I met John, my future husband, and we became friends. He was the first guy who took time to know me and not take advantage of me. He talked to me about God and His love for me. After years of searching and battling depression, I went to church with him, heard the gospel message preached for the first time, and accepted Jesus as my Lord and Savior.

About six months after surrendering my life to the Lord, I decided to go to seminary. I would love to say my trials and pain stopped, and life became glorious, but that's not the case. I developed health problems, and life became more difficult to endure. However, God showed up in miraculous ways. The healing and freedom I experienced has been worth it all, because God continues to use all things for the good of those who love Him (Romans 8:28).

While I dealt with my physical illness, I sought counseling. After years of counseling, and because of my fear to face the ugliness of my life, I hit a roadblock in healing. I decided to go to a counselor who could give spiritual guidance. For five weeks, she walked me through my life, year by year. By the time I finished telling my story, tears streamed down my face. I wasn't that person anymore.

I realized I had been trying to hide my dirtiness, shame, and unworthiness from God. By building walls around my soul, I was protecting myself from being rejected by Him. I couldn't bear for Him to leave me as well.

The night I exposed the last detail of my life to the counselor, my husband and I went to a Chris Tomlin/Big Daddy Weave concert. I was an emotional wreck, but God showed up. Big Daddy Weave sang, "Redeemed." When he sang the chorus about how he'd been called unworthy all his life, how God set him free, and he is not who he used to be, I wept. In that moment, God gave me a vision of a rainbow. He said, *Do you see this? My covenant is covering you—protecting you. You have been redeemed in Me. I do not see you as that person, and I never have. My promises are for you.*

God met me in my brokenness, just like He met the woman caught in adultery (John 8:1–11). He said, *I love you. You are redeemed.* My face immediately went from looking downward to looking at God straight in the eyes. He said, *You are not alone. Precious daughter, I love you. There is nothing you have done, been through, or will ever go through that will separate Me from you. I will not think less of you or consider you unworthy. You are My child, whom I love, and I am well pleased. You are Mine. Take My hand, and let Me speak life, love, and healing into you. Let Me help you stand up again.* That night, He spoke healing and transformation into my shattered and dying soul.

My chains were unlocked, and I was set free. The clips that held my wings were clipped off, and I began to soar. For the first time, I was no longer ashamed to say I was molested as a child, that I had vivid, explicit nightmares of my father raping me, that I abused drugs to take away gnawing pain, and that I used sex to find my identity and love. I faced the fact that I had been date-raped twice, and that all I saw while looking in the mirror was a dirty, ugly girl who couldn't bear to be in her own skin. God brought me to solid ground so I could soar higher than I ever thought possible.

Later, when God again met me at my point of need, He said, *Precious child, you have placed Me in a box. You need to hold on to the passion and vision I have placed inside your heart, and you must know that everything you have experienced will be used to bless and heal others. Yes, I did perform miracles here on Earth. I healed the sick. I cast out demons. I raised the dead, and many turned their lives over to God, but that wasn't My greatest ministry. In My pain, while being betrayed in the garden of Gethsemane, I still showed the power of God by healing a man's ear. On the cross, I asked the Father to forgive all who were persecuting Me. I never wavered in Who I was or to Whom I belonged. I stayed faithful to My Father's promises, as have you. However, Alison, it was on the cross, my darkest hour, when I was being persecuted, when My flesh was removed from the horrendous beating I took, when I was naked, with My hands and feet nailed to the cross, and when the enemy tried to shame Me, that I had My greatest ministry. It is through My crucifixion that you and others are saved and have life. The cross is what brings everyone hope, light, life, redemption, forgiveness, grace, and the ultimate sacrifice of love.*

Breathe that in. His darkest hour turned into His greatest ministry.

I still have a journey to walk in my healing, and some walls still need to be broken down. However, we are all on a journey,

126

and there are days when we get the wind knocked out of us. Visions, images, smells, touch—all trigger us, and there are days we can hardly breathe. But in those days we choose to have joy in the Lord. We choose hope in Him, because we know He will never reject us, abandon us, shame us, or make us feel dirty or unworthy. He will shower us with an unfathomable amount of love, peace, mercy, and grace. He will reach His hand out every single time and pull us out of the fire. He will bring us out of the treacherous water. He will meet us on the ground and look straight into our eyes. He will speak love and hope into our souls, and we will be transformed.

God is good all the time. Allow Him to tear down the walls and bring healing. Let Him embrace you, hold you, carry you, and lavish you with His undeniable love.

__Alison Vorlicky__ is the founder of Wrecked to Redeemed Ministries, a non-denominational, non-profit Christian ministry that empowers youth and adults seeking spiritual growth, healing, and restoration through Bible studies, speaking, writing, retreats, coaching, and mentoring. Alison has a master's degree from Ashland Theological Seminary and is married to John. She and John have two daughters and a son. Contact her at __WreckedToRedeemed.org__.

Thoughts to Ponder

from Tearing Down the Walls

1. We should seek Christian counsel when we find ourselves in deep despair.

2. There is no darkness that Jesus cannot overcome.

3. God can heal the wounds of the past and make us whole again.

What old wound of yours needs to be exposed to Jesus' light?

He heals the brokenhearted and binds up their wounds. — Psalm 147:3

Out of Control
by Brad Ross

On May 26, 1975, thrill specialist and stunt performer Evel Knievel attempted an unfathomable feat at London's Wembley Stadium. Using his motorcycle as his mode of transportation, Knievel prepared to jump over thirteen buses.

I was a young boy, glued to the console television, sitting Indian style on the shag carpet. "Would Evel make it, or would he fail?" That was the question I asked, along with the millions watching. As some may remember, the ending was both good and bad. With precision and control, Knievel miraculously cleared the buses, but on landing he lost control and crashed violently. Knievel spent eleven days in the hospital recovering from his injuries, and it was a while before he was back in action. That day, Evel's stunt burned an indelible image into my mind of "control" versus "out of control"—my first recollection of what would be a life-long compulsion to control things. Watching Knievel finish with a flop fed my fear of not being in control, as well as a fear of failure.

That same year, I experienced a situation out of my control when I watched the violent crash and dissolution of my parents' marriage. I witnessed dysfunction through rage and physical anger. Their divorce brought an *endless* list of decisions that were also out of my control.

I morphed into the textbook latch-key kid, a Gen-Xer, coupled with preoccupied divorced parents. That translated into freedom to explore and experiment with everything—with the expert guidance of a stepbrother and sisters. You name it, and I probably tried it. I witnessed the "destructive control" of the choices I made.

Fast forward to the mid-1980s, when I compared myself to my classmates. I was disappointed with the image I had created. I decided to spend more time with friends who seemed to have a purpose. However, I chose them because they appeared to be better-dressed, smarter, and wittier. They had something I did not have. By process of elimination, I saw that church was missing in my schedule, so I attended services with friends. This was my first step in "image control." During an altar call, I recognized the missing "peace" (pun intended), which was free upon accepting the gift of salvation through our Savior Jesus.

My heart and my mouth said, "Absolutely. Yes!"

That began my walk and transformation from controller into being controlled, allowing Jesus to take control. I abandoned my destructive friends and purposed to maintain this new Christian life. This was Image Control 2.0.

Romans 12:2–3 says, "Do not conform to the pattern of this world, but be transformed by the renewing of your mind. Then you will be able to test and approve what God's will is—his good, pleasing and perfect will." This new attitude changed my behavior and my life's course—at least for a while.

In 1989, after miserably failing a year in college and then working in construction, I had the opportunity to give college another try. Motivated by paying for it myself, I took my education more seriously and applied "course control."

As I focused on my career interests in the arts, I let my guard down and adopted some creative interpretations of what it meant to be a Christian—an open door to many destructive habits and a loss of my spiritual commitment. I convinced myself that my high school decision to follow Christ was an uneducated, immature experience—and I walked away.

This "educated control" is what I call *uneducated.*

In college, I met a young woman and lived with her until she gave me the ultimatum: "Marry me, or it's over." Against the advice of my college counselor, we tied the knot—but very loosely and without Christ at the center. I had effectively handed over "total control" to my new nemesis wife.

In 1999, after having brought two boys into the world, I swore that I would never put my sons through what I had experienced with my parents' divorce. I once heard that if you focus on what you want to avoid, you are guaranteed to hit it head on.

Nine years later, my wife and I painfully realized that marriage had not been a wise decision, and it might not work out. During one of my overseas trips, she packed up the boys and moved to Dallas. I returned to an empty house, where I collapsed, out of control.

Have you ever seen the little arrow on a map that points to failure, saying, "You are here"? My failure was fully realized. I can still hear the words coming from my mouth: "Nothing good can come out of this."

Over the next few years, I came to understand what that arrow meant. I also learned the most important meaning of that phrase in relation to Jesus. He said, "You are here, but so am I," and "I love you, no matter what."

I had abandoned our relationship, but He had not abandoned me. He was there when no one on Earth could help me. Not Mom. Not Dad. Not my sister. Not a counselor. No one.

In 2 Corinthians 12, the apostle Paul spoke about a "thorn in his flesh" that plagued him. He prayed for relief, but God said, "My grace is sufficient for you, for My power is made perfect in weakness." Paul said he would therefore gladly boast about his weaknesses so Christ's power might dwell in him. For Christ's sake, he chose to delight in weaknesses, insults, hardships, persecutions, and difficulties. In my weakness, could I be strong?

In 2003, I was living in Frisco, back in the DFW Metroplex. I had all but given up on finding a cute single girl. The city stats were clearly not in my favor. Most young women were married, and I wasn't sure anyone would be interested in a divorced dad with two boys.

But the Lord once again proved that I wasn't in control, when I visited a small start-up congregation. I heard the most beautiful voice on stage, from the mouth of a super-cute girl— as if I had been exclusively invited to join in her personal concert of praise to the Most High God.

Now, Tiffany and I have been happily married for fifteen years, with a daughter, Lily. Our two boys, Adan and Eli, are serving in the Marine Corps.

I still get emotional when my wife leads us into the pure worship of our God. I encourage it as much as possible.

I've learned that when I defer to God's control, things work out way better. I do not pretend to have mastered this, but I am getting better. The Lord keeps giving me opportunities to relinquish control, and I am quick to let go and thank Him for His grace and mercies. I've learned that if my hands are clinched around the controls, my hands are no longer open to receive. With all the insecurities and craziness in this world, I remind myself to do what I can, do it as best I can and let God control the outcome.

By the way, Evel Knievel went on to make about six more jumps after that day in England. Before he died in 2007, he made the most important jump of all when he accepted Jesus as his Lord and Savior. Once again, he did it before a crowd. Reportedly, hundreds of people accepted Jesus as Lord and Savior when Knievel was baptized at the Crystal Cathedral in Southern California. That day, he said, "Jesus Christ is everything! I know that now. If I had known that years and years ago, I would have been three times the man I thought I was."

Like me, Evel Knievel came to realize Who was in control.[1]

Brad Ross lives in Plano, Texas, with his wife, Tiffany, and their daughter, Lily. Their older sons, Adan and Eli, are currently serving in the Marine Corps. Though most of his adult career has been in the fashion industry, many people find it intriguing that, along with his sons, Brad also served in the military, the United States Army. Brad was the Head of Design at Nishat Apparel Group. In his spare time, he loves to experiment with interior design and painting. Brad is grateful to the Lord for His faithful presence in the journey.

---

[1] http://thunderstruck.org/evel-knievels-leap-of-faith/.
https://www.breakingchristiannews.com/articles/display_art.html?ID=3873.

Thoughts to Ponder
from Out of Control

1. We might think we are in control, but we are not.

2. When we take a leap of faith, it will impact others.

3. God can bring what's out of control, under control.

> **When have you felt like you were out of control?**

Come to me, all you who are weary and burdened, and I will give you rest. — Matthew 11:28

I Love That You're My Dad

by Julie Steck

"Daddy John would like to adopt you," the email read.

Adopt me at 35 ... really! With great anticipation I wondered what my mom's email actually meant.

"It means we would rightly acknowledge Daddy John as your father," my mom said, "the role he has played for thirty years now."

Tears spilled down my cheeks. I had never felt so loved.

The whole thing caught me off guard. I had never thought about being adopted. I knew my stepdad loved me and thought of me as his daughter. He demonstrated his commitment by standing with my mom and me through the tough years. So my stepdad didn't *have* to do this. He wanted to.

For weeks after I read mom's email, I processed the significance of what this meant to me. The email lingered in the back of my mind while I washed dishes and folded the laundry. *Adoption. I'm going to be adopted!*

After the court date, I would be issued a new birth certificate with my *new* maiden name, as if my original last name had never existed. I thought about my middle and high school years. My mom taught art at the school I attended, so I continually had to explain why my last name was different from hers. Even kids in the same situation didn't connect the dots and asked, "Why is your mom's last name different from yours? Is she your *real* mom?" I rolled my eyes and reminded them that if she was my stepmom, not my real mom, then I would share her last name. When she married my stepdad, her name changed. Mine didn't.

"Oh, yeah," they said.

Then I recounted the story of how my parents divorced when I was one, and my mom remarried when I was almost five.

Wow! This adoption means I don't have to explain the story of my mom's divorce anymore. Now there's closure. Daddy John isn't my stepdad. He is my dad.

Before this adoption, I wore a torn garment—like a shirt torn at the sleeve seam, evidence of our broken family. I didn't ask to wear this shirt. It was handed to me that way. My mom never wanted her divorce. She never wanted me to wear a shirt with a torn sleeve. But through that time, she grew in her knowledge and understanding of God. As a result, at age three, I saw my mom's strength and told her I wanted "her Jesus" in my heart. However, whenever I met a new friend and shared my testimony or introduced my parents, I felt the need to explain the tear. Why would I wear a torn shirt?

The problem with a torn shirt is the unraveling. Unless the tear is mended quickly, the fragile, threadbare strings will widen into a gaping hole, making the shirt unfit to wear. So it was with my torn sleeve. Entering into a second marriage with a step-parent relationship puts you automatically behind the figurative eight ball. That was something my five-year-old maturity didn't understand.

This blended family wasn't easy. God designed my stepdad and me with unique differences. Over the years, these pulled and stretched the fabric of our relationship in ways that caused the rip to widen.

How you view your earthly father can affect how you see God as your heavenly Father. For me, despite an imperfect parent situation, I saw God as my faithful heavenly Father, always taking care of me. Instead of feeling bitter that He would allow a girl to wear a shirt with a torn sleeve, I felt a sweetness, a closeness with the Lord that He was personally with me. Let's be honest, no one is a perfect parent. Our earthly parents will fail us in some way, but that should lead us to look up. In the absence of a perfect father or stepfather, God is perfect all the time and will never fail us.

I left home at eighteen, marrying the boy I met at the nearby swimming pool a few years before. The day we said "I do," I exchanged my torn garment for his last name. Now, in place of my stepdad, stood my new husband. When I boxed up my belongings, I packed away the sleeve-torn garment as well.

Now that I wasn't living under the same roof as my stepdad, our differences stopped dividing us. We found similarities to marvel in. As children were added to my family, Daddy John slipped easily into the role of grandfather. I loved watching him form relationships with my children.

Miraculously through time, tears, and humility, and through prayers, love, and grace, God has not only stopped the continual tearing, but He has patched over the areas that were once gaping holes. Still, when I bring out that garment to tell my story, I feel the need to explain the "patches."

On a Sunday evening, just as we finished watching a family movie, I opened my mom's email asking me to consider letting Daddy John adopt me. The words blurred on the screen because of my tears, and I immediately knew my answer.

Yes! Daddy John can adopt me, because after all these years, I know he has been my dad.

Through this adoption, I see redemption. After the court date, I was issued a new birth certificate stating my new maiden name. It was like my old name was erased and replaced. It was a beautiful, physical representation of 2 Corinthians 5:17: "Therefore, if anyone is in Christ, the new creation has come: The old has gone, the new is here!" Just like my stepdad chose to adopt me, Jesus chose me and has given me a new name—Redeemed. Daughter. His. This happened, not because I'm such a great kid, but because of His great love for me.

My patched-up sleeve has been gathered and woven into a seam by the red thread of His redemption. In the process, God didn't remove the patches. Like a master weaver, He smoothly wove His thread in, around, and through all the piled-up, messy layers. He closed the gap. He mended the tear. He soothed the hurt. He forgave the mistakes. Ultimately, He redeemed the story.

Julie Steck, a native East Texan, met her husband, Adam, on the banks of the neighborhood trailer park pool, where she worked as the pool attendant. They married two years later at the ripe old age of eighteen. Today, they own Southwest Steel Buildings in Mineola while raising their three kids, Caleb, Mackenzie, and Zach. When not writing, Julie enjoys date nights at Wasabi, supporting overseas missionaries, staring at the mountains in Colorado, and remodeling her kitchen over the holidays. Find her book, No More Secrets: Set Free from Fear, Shame and Control by Discovering True Grace, *or follow her blog at* **JulieSteck.com.**

Thoughts to Ponder
from I Love That You're My Dad

1. God is the perfect Father.

2. Our brokenness doesn't scare God.

3. We are adopted into God's family through Jesus Christ.

> ### **What has God redeemed in your life?**

The Spirit you received does not make you slaves . . . rather, the Spirit you received brought about your adoption to sonship. And by him we cry, "Abba, Father." — Romans 8:15

Blessed Assurance
by Shelley Allen

Have you ever had a relationship with a family member that was strained? You never knew what they would say or what they would do? Did you live with that person?

I had a scenario like that as I attempted to maneuver through my childhood, trying to please my mother. My mother was strict, harsh, tyrannical. Every moment spent in her presence was filled with fear of her near-constant physical, verbal, and psychological attacks. "I would have aborted you if abortion had been legal back then," she told us. Her words often stung far worse—and far longer—than her slaps, punches, pinches, beatings, and kicks ever did.

My little sister, Lynn, and I often played outside and in the park. In the days when children were seldom abducted, we walked for miles, from daylight to dark, all over Manitou Springs, Colorado. In the park one summer day, when we were seven and eight, some sweet people invited Lynn and me to their church for Vacation Bible School (VBS).

To get us out of her hair, Mom allowed us to go. During VBS, we were treated kindly and learned about Jesus. So with the faith of a child, I accepted Jesus as my Lord and Savior at the age of eight. I became a child with an unexpected, peaceful disposition. Many people commented, wondering why I was calmer and quieter than my sister and mother. While they were loud, obscene, vulgar, and bitter, I was quiet and thoughtful. I did not use coarse language, and I treated everyone respectfully. Why? I believe the Holy Spirit filled my heart with faith and hope. I developed an eternal perspective, comforted by the promise shared in the old hymn, "Blessed assurance, Jesus is mine! O, what a foretaste of glory divine!"

Throughout the rest of my childhood, I clung to the promises I had received while going to church. Though my mother was hateful, violent, and left no doubt that she did not want us, I believed God loved me and wanted me, and I thanked Him often for blessings large and small. His Spirit nurtured in me a thankful heart, one that did not become bitter despite the abuse. I give Him full glory and honor for that.

I embraced God as my Father more tightly, because I didn't have an earthly one. Divorced from my mother by the time I was seven, my blood father rarely had anything to do with us, and the man we lived with, my common-law dad, Jim, wasn't very affectionate. He was often away, working, and though we lived off-and-on with him for ten years, I never thought of him as a father figure.

During our teenage years, Mom's abuse worsened, and I clung more firmly to the faith I had in God's goodness, for I was blessed with occasional kindnesses from strangers, teachers, and a few friends. Unfortunately, Lynn's personality made it so she rarely, if ever, received such gestures or affirmations. She struggled in school, made very few friends, and bore the brunt of Mom's anger more often than I did—because she never learned how to guard her mouth.

Mother was abusive, not only to Lynn and me but also to our stepbrother, Jimmy. One horrifying day, all I could do was sob helplessly in fear and sympathy for Jimmy, age fifteen, as Mom beat him, wrapped her legs around his neck, and then banged his head numerous times into the solid wood wall of his bedroom. I thought she was going to kill him.

Not long after that, I ran away from home. I walked eleven miles, following train tracks in the cold, February darkness. Once again, God protected me and provided for me. I was sixteen and walked up to a stranger, a trucker at a truck stop, and asked if I could get a ride in his Mrs. Baird's truck to Texas. He said yes, so I climbed into his sleeper cab and fell asleep while he finished his rounds.

I learned in the morning that he had taken me in the opposite direction, to his home in Pueblo, Colorado. Thank God the man was a kind Christian, and his wife, his children, and his church family accepted, comforted, and encouraged me. Their behavior strengthened my belief that God was watching over me, protecting and caring for me. Because I had been protected, I trusted God even more.

After a few days, the Witt family convinced me to call my mother. Mom promised she would get some counseling for me, because rather than tell her I ran away because of her abuse, I told her I had run away because I felt I was going crazy and needed counseling. Mr. Witt took me back home.

But my mother lied. She mocked me for wanting counseling. The next spring, when I was a junior in high school, I came up with a plan to escape my mother for good. I wrote to her mother, my grandmother, in Texas, asking if I could live with her during my senior year so I could become eligible to pay in-state-resident tuition when I entered college after graduation. My mother believed the ruse and allowed me to live with Grandma. She drove me to Texas in June, threatening to take me back throughout the trip, even after I settled in.

With me out of the home, my mother's abuse of Lynn grew worse, until finally Child Protective Services removed Lynn from the home that fall. Lynn subsequently endured thirty years of suffering and abuse at the hands of many. She made poor decisions, resulting in a cycle of poverty, depression, addiction, and homelessness, culminating in her suicide five years ago. I have tried not to blame my mother for my sister's suicide, but it is hard because I believe it was my mother who had mortally wounded Lynn's self-image, self-esteem, and self-respect to the point that she told me once in her twenties, "Mom hated and beat me, so why shouldn't they?" She was speaking of all the men who had abused her.

Our stepbrother, Jimmy, made decisions leading to a lifestyle of drug use, alcoholism, and poverty. He died last year at just forty-nine, and to be honest, I haven't had the courage to write and ask his children, whom I've never met, what caused his death. I believe my mother's treatment of him caused much of his lifelong anguish and suffering.

Early in my senior year of high school, I met Gary. We married in June, before I turned eighteen in August, and lived five years happily married. I felt God had blessed me, was taking care of me. I believed God loved me even though I was not serving Him directly.

While living with Grandma, I had attended church, and I began to miss it as a young married woman. I missed worshipping God in fellowship with others. We visited several churches, and when I was almost thirty, we joined a nondenominational church in a small town east of Dallas. We raised our children in that grace-filled, loving church family over the next sixteen years.

While attending that Bible church, I learned the most about Job. When I studiously contemplated his assertion, "Though He slay me, yet will I hope in Him" (Job 13:15), I felt the words echo, reverberate, and rumble within, as if they had been rung from a heavy bell in the deepest recesses of my heart.

My God is worthy of such faith. He has proven to me to be trustworthy, has always taken care of me and provided for me, so I would trust Him no matter what, even if He were to decide to slay me.

I rededicated my life to Christ during the time we attended Country Bible Church, and I enjoyed serving Him through numerous ministries. As the years went by, I grew more unhappy in my marriage. I tried to ignore my unhappiness. I plowed through the years and silent tears, burying myself in chores, distracting myself with tasks, and hoping my discontentment would heal or go away.

I bore my unhappiness quietly. After all, Job was my hero, and my life motto was, "Though He slay me, yet will I hope in Him." I trusted my Father amid blessing and joy, so I trusted Him also in the face of trials, pain, and suffering. Still, because of my sinful heart, I began to wander from God. I believed I was serving Him through the church, through my service to my family, and later through my Christian bookstore, but I became more unhappy still, more selfish and self-centered. I persevered as my hero Job did, but I became worse at doing it.

After twenty-five years of marriage, I chose to divorce my husband. In the eight years since, I have never forgotten that I need forgiveness for the sins I commit daily. Jesus' death paid for all of the times I have disappointed and disobeyed God—all of them, from the time I was a child to the ones I commit even now. If I had not agreed to accept Jesus' willing sacrifice as payment for the debt I owe the One and Only Sovereign God, I would still be in debt to my Creator. God loves me. He has always loved me, and I will die believing He loves me, for He has proven time and time again that He does. If I had not received the gift He offered to me—and to you—I would not have this hope I have now, the blessed assurance that Jesus' gift is mine, and I am His.

He willingly gave Himself up, suffered the pain, shame, and horror of being crucified so you and I could live for all eternity in the presence of the loving, kind God, my only true Father. When we accept Him and His gift, we receive the Holy Spirit, Who comforts us and teaches us. He guides us and strengthens us, supplying us with everything we need to live for our Father, Who loves us so much He gave His only begotten Son, that whosoever would believe in Him would have everlasting life.

I may not understand what or why something is happening, but I know *the Who* behind all that is happening, and God is merciful, good, and trustworthy. My Father provides for me. My Father comforts me. My Father cares for me. My Father carries me. My Father blesses me continually. He always has, and He always will. I hope you will accept His gift and rest in Him—in this blessed assurance—as I have.

__Shelley Allen__ is a mother to four and grandmother to five. In her forties, Shelley earned her Master's in Secondary Education at SMU and taught high school English Language Arts in Carrollton, Texas. In June 2018, Shelley resigned from teaching and became a freelance copy editor and writer. In addition to editing books, articles, web content, and myriad other documents, Shelley has written articles and various other manuscripts for businesses, individuals, and entrepreneurs worldwide. She has also written a biography/math history book on Leonardo Pisano (aka Fibonacci), which is available on Amazon. It is titled Master Fibonacci: The Man Who Changed Math. *Her website is __RuthlessRedPen.com.__*

Thoughts to Ponder
from Blessed Assurance

1. In a hostile situation, God can give us peace.

2. We can be assured that God is with us.

3. God is trustworthy in every situation.

How have you trusted God during oppression?

Though He slay me,
yet will I hope in Him. — Job 13:15

The Miracle Day

by Lorraine Lorio Besson

Have you ever thought you would experience a miracle in your life? Well, I had not, but that is exactly what happened.

It has been said, "It takes a village to raise a child." I said, "It took Jesus and a highly specialized team of medical professionals to help save my life on March 20th, 2016." Miracles are recognized by the extraordinary measure of God revealing Himself to us. Luke 18:27 says, "What is impossible with man is possible with God." Many miracles were performed on my behalf that day. Friends said Jesus was not yet ready to take me to Heaven. He had more work for me to do.

The following is an account of what happened on Friday, March 18, and Sunday, March 20, 2016. My neurosurgeon, Dr. Paul Waguespack, told me I needed a very common cervical-spinal-fusion surgery. Otherwise, I might become paralyzed. The MRI showed arthritic bony spurs pressing my spinal column, crushing my spinal cord in three places.

After four hours of major surgery and twenty-three hours of recovery, I was sent home. Complications from all the strong medications caused retrograde amnesia. I couldn't remember going to the hospital two days before or anything else that happened until after five days following surgery. My doctor said this occurs to less than .5 percent of those who have the surgery.

On Sunday, two days after my surgery, I awakened at 3:00 a.m. with horrific pain in my left leg, hurting so bad that I vomited. No doctor ever told me what caused that pain. Nurses have said it could have been a blood clot that broke off after my surgery. If so, I thank God that it didn't travel to my heart, lungs, or brain and kill me. My husband, Bob, told me the pain subsided, and I went back to sleep.

The next morning, my loving son, Brian, came to check on me. He said I was coughing a little while trying to eat. I didn't appear to be in any great distress, and he left. Shortly thereafter, I asked Bob to please call 9-1-1, because I couldn't breathe. He told me to sit down, and I said, "I don't know why, but I can't."

144

He said I wasn't panicking. I was calm. He called 9-1-1, and they asked him to tell me to sit down, which I couldn't do. Nurses have told me why. When I was sitting, my internal organs were scrunched up, making it harder to breathe. When I was standing, my lungs could expand, making it easier to breathe.

Paramedics put me on the stretcher and placed me in the ambulance. They said I was sitting up and talking to them. Bob followed behind, thinking he might need his car at the hospital. I believe God helped him make that decision. What happened to me in the ambulance would have been very traumatic for him. While I was being transported, I coded twice. After arriving at the hospital, I coded again in the trauma room. While there is no formal definition for a code, doctors often use the term as slang to refer to a patient in cardiopulmonary arrest. I had no heart or lung function and required a physician to begin immediate resuscitative efforts to establish an airway for breathing.

The first miracle of my story is that there was someone unexpected in the ambulance—besides Jesus, the angels, and a paramedic—an emergency room doctor. The only thing keeping me alive was emergency procedures that this doctor performed daily. Dr. Martin Blake initiated CPR on me. EMS paramedic, Jeremy Landry, tried to get an airway, but was unsuccessful. Somehow, my family arrived at the hospital before the ambulance. My daughter said, "Mom, I never want to see anything like that again. When they threw open the doors of the ambulance, we just knew you were dead." My hands were dangling off the stretcher, and the doctor was performing CPR.

In the ER, Dr. Lura Wight worked on me for thirty minutes in the trauma room, trying to establish an airway, but she was unsuccessful. She called an anesthesiologist, Dr. Alex Aitken. He had a special scope that no one else had and was finally successful intubating me—the insertion of a breathing tube into the trachea for mechanical ventilation. I was put on a ventilator, taken to surgery, placed in a drug-induced coma, and was then moved to the Intensive Care Unit (ICU).

My loving daughter arranged a schedule so someone from my family or friends was with me at all times. God bless her. Many family members and friends lifted me up in prayer. After five days in ICU, I was taken off the ventilator and spent the next five days recovering from the trauma I had endured.

I was then moved to the neurological floor for observation. After several days, the Medical Director of the Inpatient Rehabilitation Unit, Dr. Martin Setliff, admitted me. When I later met him, he said, "Mrs. Besson, when you first presented to me on the rehab unit, I was amazed how well you were doing, given all you went through. I was concerned about long-term brain injury, but after a short time in the unit, I felt recovery was a real possibility. You worked hard, persevered through a very difficult situation, and recovered as well as could be expected." One of my physical therapists on the unit also said he couldn't believe how quickly I recovered after being on the ventilator.

Something very special happened to me one day when I was alone in my hospital room. I began crying softly. I didn't hear an audible voice from God, but I found myself saying, "Why me, Lord? Why me? Why would you choose me to help spread your Word of salvation to the people?"

When Jesus makes you bold, you become bold for Him. A doctor told me that God had prepared my whole life for what was going to happen that day. I had always tried hard to be that "good little Catholic girl," and I think I was. I sang in the children's choir, went to Confraternity of Christian Doctrine classes, was baptized, made my First Communion and Confirmation, and was married in the Catholic church.

On the twenty-fourth day, I walked out of that hospital without any major brain damage—a miracle. I went through four-and-a-half months of outpatient physical therapy. The therapists were very encouraging and helped me even when I didn't think I could go on any longer.

Several months later, I wanted to meet the people who contributed to saving me. First I met EMS paramedic Jeremy Landry. My son, Brian, had worked with him before and told Jeremy I wanted to meet him. So my husband and I took him to lunch. Jeremy is a very fine young man. I asked him what the chances were of having a doctor, much less an ER doctor, in my ambulance.

"Mrs. Besson," he said, "the chances were slim to none."

For whatever reason, he was in there, and I think it was

preordained by God. I praise Jesus for this first miracle.

The second person we took to lunch was ER Dr. Martin Blake. He was quiet while eating. I couldn't help but wonder what he was thinking. He finally said, "Mrs. Besson, I can't believe I'm eating lunch with you today, knowing what I know happened to you. And you don't have major brain damage." I cried softly, as this was a very emotional time for me to be with another person who helped save me.

When I met with ER Dr. Lura Wight, I was so excited that I almost felt giddy. She came out from the ER to talk with me, and I was immediately overwhelmed with emotion, in awe to be with another person who had helped me. All I wanted to do was hug her and thank her, but she had so much more she wanted to say. She must have thought I was a strong person, because she started recalling all that had happened.

"Mrs. Besson," she said, "I never thought I'd see you walk through the doors of this hospital. You were every doctor's worst nightmare that day. No one, absolutely no one in the trauma room, could get an airway for you."

Someone told my family that there were so many people in the trauma room, they had to ask some to leave.

Dr. Wight said, "I was just getting ready to pick up the scalpel to do a tracheotomy on you. I did not hear an audible voice, but something told me *Stop, don't do the tracheotomy.*

A tracheotomy is an incision made in the windpipe to relieve an obstruction to breathing. I knew Who that *something* was— Jesus Christ. I am weeping as I say this, because I realize just how very close I came to death that day. Thank God that Dr. Wight listened to the "still small voice of God." Shortly after, she found out what was wrong. I had developed a thyroid arterial bleed that was caused by my vomiting, due to the pain in my leg. The bleeding had formed a large hematoma or blood clot that was pressing on my airway, making me unable to breathe.

"Mrs. Besson," Dr. Wight said, "if I had picked up that scalpel and performed a tracheotomy, you would have bled out and died because of that blood clot. I thought you were going to be a vegetable for the rest of your life." She then described a third miracle on March 20. "I was not the only person who helped save you that day." She called in anesthesiologist, Dr. Alex Aitken, who was finally able to establish an airway.

With the help of a very special young lady, I looked forward to meeting Dr. Aitkin.

As my husband and I were eating dinner later that evening, the phone rang. I could hardly believe it. Dr. Aitkin was calling. Overwhelmed with joy, I began crying and asked if he remembered me. "Yes," he said, "how could I forget you?" We decided to meet the following week at the hospital. When a young doctor came walking toward me, I just knew who he was. I asked if I could hug him. As you might imagine, I will never forget that moment.

I met with neurosurgeon Dr. Richard A. Stanger, who was the doctor who took me to surgery to remove the blood clot. "Mrs. Besson," he said, "I am glad I was in the right place at the right time to help you."

After recovery, I returned to my church and asked Fr. Tom what Jesus was asking me to do. "Just live," he said. I thanked him and left, not knowing what that meant. So the following week, I asked him, and he said, "Just live your life."

I wanted to give all the people who had helped save my life a special gift. I found four beautiful standing crosses at the Hallmark store. The next day I wanted another one for me. I could look at it on the mantle in my den and remember who helped save my life that day, besides Jesus. I later gave Dr. Stanger and Dr. Setliff their crosses.

Besides my daughter Sheri, her husband, David, and their sons, Tyler, Alex, Brent, Brian, Brice, and my son Brian, his wife, Rachel, and their daughters, Olivia, Elizabeth, and Elena Grace, there are eight other very important people in my life. Jesus Christ, who gave me life in the beginning and then saved my life on March 20, 2016. I am grateful for Bob, my husband, who is the love of my life, as well as Dr. Martin Blake, Dr. Lura Wight, Dr. Alex Atkin, Dr. Richard A. Stanger, and paramedic Jeremy Landry. Dr. Martin Setliff helped restore me to my former physical health. Let me not forget to thank all the wonderful ICU nurses and other nurses and staff who took excellent care of me. Thank you, Jesus, for all these special people.

When I first woke up from the drug-induced coma, everyone asked me the same question. "Had I seen the white light, Jesus, or Heaven?" I always felt bad, because I had to answer no. I hadn't seen any of those things. A friend said, "Lorraine, you could have very well seen all those things and more, and just not remember them. After all, you don't even remember going to the hospital two days before the surgery or the five days following the surgery."

After this discussion, my prayer on Saturday night, the day before Easter Sunday, March 27, 2018, was this: "Dear Lord Jesus, if I saw You at any of the three times I coded on March 20, 2016, would You please let me know?"

On Easter Sunday, April 1, 2018, I had a "vision" while sitting in church. A vision is an experience of seeing someone or something in a dream or trance or a supernatural apparition. I don't know how long it lasted, because I was totally unaware of what was going on around me. I noticed light coming through one of the beautiful stained glass windows. As I was looking, it turned into the most brilliant white, radiating light that I had ever seen. Bob said I saw the sunlight. Shortly thereafter, two small white crosses appeared at the bottom of this white light. Somehow, I knew that this was "the resurrection of Jesus." Darkness began to appear in the center of the white light. I looked down at my hands and noticed that my thumbs had turned dark red. I didn't really understand what that meant. It scared me so much that I tapped Bob on the shoulder and asked if my thumbs were red. He said, "No, Lorraine, your thumbs are not red." At first, I didn't quite understand what I was seeing. After a while, I realized that I had seen the "crucifixion of Jesus," because of the darkness, the death, the red, and the blood of Jesus shed on the cross. I was shocked by what had happened. As I was walking to my car after Mass, I recorded on my phone what I had seen. I tried to make sense of it, but I didn't understand why I would see Jesus' resurrection before Jesus' crucifixion.

I began telling people what had happened and about my not understanding the vision. They shared their interpretation of what it meant to them. There was one explanation that I believed was true. It was that Jesus showed me His resurrection before His crucifixion so that when the darkness of my death would come, I would not be frightened. I would realize that I had nothing to fear. After all, Jesus died on the cross for my sins so I could have everlasting life with God in Heaven.

I have shared my miracle story many times. I felt privileged when I was asked to speak in December 2016 to the patients of the Inpatient Rehabilitation Unit, where I had been nine months before. They wanted me to give patients hope for their recovery. I have told my story at the supermarket, the medical center where I volunteer, my church, and with small and large groups. I even shared it at my local movie theater. My favorite way to share is with individuals that I often feel God is leading me to.

One of the most meaningful encounters I had was with a young man working in the medical center cafeteria. I asked him if I could share my miracle story, and he said yes. He was very quiet. As I moved down the serving line, I heard him say in a soft voice, "I have to get back to church." I actually jumped back, his words moved me so much. I asked what he meant, and he said his best friend had been murdered three weeks before. He hadn't been able to sleep since then. My heart broke for him. I checked back with him to see how he was, and he was doing well. Praise you, Jesus.

One day I stood up in the movie theater after watching a Christian movie. I was crying and turned to ask if anyone would like to hear my miracle story. Someone said yes, so I shared it. These people were from a church in north Baton Rouge. The pastor said, "We're the ones nobody wants. We are from zip code 70805." This is one of the areas where so many of the murders were taking place. "I am the pastor," he said, "and I have the choir director and the choir with me today." After telling my story, we went outside on the steps of the theater, held hands, and prayed for our community. The ladies prayed for their young men to "put down their guns and stop the killings." This was a very moving experience for me, and I felt the power of God working in this situation.

Writing this account of my miracle story has been very emotional for me. It's been three years since my miracle day occurred, but it seems like it was only yesterday. I choose not to live in the past, although I will never forget it. Nor do I wish to live in the future. I strive to live for this day only. Sometimes I stumble and fall, but God picks me up, and I start over again.

Celebrate your life, because you never know when it will be your last day. The Lord knows it was almost mine. Don't let that scare you, because I say, "It's a new day every day in Heaven with God and the angels." What more could a person ask for?

Lorraine Lorio Besson *is a seventy-year-old native of Baton Rouge, Louisiana, married to her husband, Bob, for forty-eight years. Her daughter, Sheri, and her husband, David, have five boys: Tyler, Alex, Brent, Brian and Brice. Her son, Brian, and his wife, Rachel, have three daughters: Olivia, Elizabeth, and Elena Grace. She is retired from the East Baton Rouge Parish public school system as a Special Education paraprofessional. She has been a Catholic Christian all her life. Her miracle day that changed her life forever occurred on March 20, 2016.*

Thoughts to Ponder
from The Miracle Day

1. Miracles still happen every day.

2. God can provide a miracle for you.

3. We are not guaranteed tomorrow.

**When have you
experienced a miracle?**

*Jesus replied, "What is impossible with man
is possible with God." — Luke 18:27*

Just like Mary Poppins
by Vickie Lubbock

How many of you have heard the amazing story of Mary
Poppins? You can call me her twin—without the umbrella. I
have been a nanny for thirty-one years, loving other people's
kids, singing to them and playing with them. I've been recruited
by doctors, lawyers, movie stars, engineers and even a Louisiana
senator.

I have been called the Pied Piper. People say, if I played a
flute, all the kids would follow me out of town.

I grew up loving kids.

As a young girl I spent all my time in church. We had regular
revivals where the evangelist stayed for weeks. I got close to
each family by loving and taking care of their kids. I loved all the
kids, babysitting for many in the church. Over time, these
activities naturally steered me into becoming a professional
nanny.

Although I loved kids, I'd never been able to have any of my
own. In my very early twenties, I married a man recommended
by my pastor. Surprisingly, we didn't have any children. Like too
many young marrieds, things did not work out. After five years,
my husband asked for a divorce.

My church's beliefs were strict, and I knew I wouldn't be able
to remarry if I stayed in that church. Worse, I was taught that as
a divorcee, God wouldn't allow me to have assurance of
spending eternity with God, especially if I remarried. That
would be adultery, an unforgivable sin.

I was so young, and I wanted to remarry one day—to the
right man. So I chose to leave the church. The next step for a
"lost girl" coming from an overly restrictive life is pretty easy to
guess: I stepped right in to the partying scene, looking for love
in the wrong places. My earnest hope was to find a guy to marry
me, "Mr. Right."

I was just a child when my father divorced my mother. She
was left penniless living with eight kids in a trailer. Dad was
never in my life. When seeking a man's love, I did what so many
young women do: I got pregnant—a twenty-six-year-old single

woman. *Wow! Not me. This couldn't be.* Single and pregnant, away from my family and church, I was freaking out. There was absolutely no way I could go back to Mom. Looking for answers and help, I called a few people for advice. They encouraged me to think about abortion. *Oh, my gosh! Not me. Not ever.* So I called my mom and told her I was coming home.

Before I took that step, I again counseled with the wrong people. I was desperate to escape what I was facing. Uniformly, they encouraged me to have an abortion. At that point, I just wore out and became emotionally bankrupt. I went numb about the whole deal. Mustering up courage to take action, I called my big sister and said, "Come get me," asking her to take me to the clinic. Knowing my love for kids, she told me this was out of character for me. She asked me to wait and think on it. The loss of any future life for me was too strong a torment to overcome. I called her back and said, "Let's do it."

Remember, I was raised without a dad in our home and suffered terribly. My own hurt was still with me, and I did not want my child to go through this life without a father. My sister reluctantly picked me up and took me to the abortion clinic. We did it on a Friday, and I didn't even know it was Mother's Day weekend. It was a horrible experience.

Hurting, confused, and very lonely, I went back into the barroom scene. Looking back, I can see that I was running and hiding from God. There was no escaping the knowledge that I had sinned against God by taking my baby's life. As I looked for life, escape, and a man to love me, I met the wrong kind of men. Very wrong. The man I hoped would love me raped me instead.

A relationship was so important to me that I moved into a guy's home when I knew he was unstable. This part of my story was far from a Mary Poppins tale. The guy used me and let me support him as his source for drug money. I remained with him because I feared being alone. He pulled a gun on me and let a stream of bullets fly over my head as I sought to break away. Bad turned to worse when he tried to stick the gun barrel down my throat. I managed to flee for my life.

Fast forward a few months. I met this gorgeous man named Mark. After his own brief struggle, he gave his life to God and told me he was temporarily abandoning relationships to spend time learning about how to live as a Christian. Not wanting to miss this opportunity, I chased him as he went back to church.

He said to me, "If God takes me home before you, then I'll be there waiting in New Jerusalem for you at the South Wall and East Gate." He referred to the scripture teaching that when Jesus returns, there will be a new city of Jerusalem coming down from Heaven to Earth.

I told him, "No! Don't say that." I was terribly scared of death. Sin like mine could only lead to bad consequences for all eternity, and the mere thought of that terrified me. What I didn't know at the time was that God had a unique personal experience awaiting me, which would change my heart and mind regarding death.

In the third year of our dating, I went to bed and had an out-of-body experience where I died. As the scene unfolded, I was with familiar church ladies and my mom, in a pit that started filling with water. I was going to drown. It seemed so real. I left my body and floated up to halfway between Heaven and Hell. My body below was no more than dirt and dust. Next, I was in midair but could hear screaming below. Looking down, I saw that I was holding onto my mother's hand while I was holding a baby in the other arm. "God," I cried, "*please* let me go with You and not to Hell."

Raised with very strong restrictions, I was taught that most things I had done as a young girl would send me to Hell. While floating in the air, I begged God to let me know if I was saved. Praise God! I floated up instead of down. The bright light that everyone talks about was in front of me—a bright, white light. As I drifted toward it, I let go of Mom's hand. I entered this incredible place where the peace cannot be described. I then let go of the baby in my arm. Waters were running. I heard indescribable singing, prettier than the most angelic voices on Earth. I was saved from eternal death. I saw a form on a big throne, and I knew it was God. I felt His presence. I knew this was God showing me about my own salvation. It was *not* too late.

I told Him thank You and asked Him to please let me stay there. The wildest thing is that I had been obsessed with a man down on Earth, but I didn't care about that. I never wanted to leave the peace of Heaven.

As I slowly drifted down toward my body, God said, "Go back and tell them."

The lady that I lived with heard my moaning as I tossed and turned in my sleep. She and her daughter came to my bedside, very concerned. They said my experience lasted for a few hours. Watching over me, they kept adding blankets to warm me, because I was violently shivering even though the heat was on. They said my extreme body movements were like I was convulsing.

All the way down, I begged God not to make me go, but He kept saying with a loud voice, "Go back and tell them."

As I struggled to wake up, I said, "He made me come back. He made me come back!"

My friends did not know God, and they did not understand. They said my face was glowing.

Going into my body was difficult, kind of like the movie *Ghost*. Wow!

The next time I saw my love, I told him, "Okay, I'm ready to meet you at the South Wall and East Gate!" He shed tears as I told him of my experience. I wasn't afraid of death anymore. Thank God.

By my love's side, I drew closer to God, and we got married. He became a pastor, and I served as the "first lady" for fifteen years. During this time, I had several emotional break-downs. I cried uncontrollably, knowing that I had allowed my baby to have its life taken away, and I could never get pregnant again. Attempting to move forward, I used my gift of love for children to bless other families. The next ten years were so hard, but my love was awesome by always being there for me. Pouring my heart into serving others through ministry also helped my sanity.

While at a small group one night, I was crying and telling them about my out-of-body experience. My dear sister in Christ turned to me and said, "Oh, Vickie! God just showed me that the baby in your arms was the baby you aborted. God took it home when you released it as you were going up." I took that comfort to heart.

Soon after that, I experienced another "God thing" when I found out about an upcoming retreat for people who had had abortions. First, a friend mentioned it to me. Without knowing this, my husband pointed out a story in the newspaper about the same retreat. I quickly sent my application for one of the spaces.

For the first time ever, I got to acknowledge my baby. They took me through an exercise where I was able to name her. They gave me a certificate—a life certificate saying she was in Heaven. This was my journey in healing, in accepting God's love and forgiveness.

Of course, God knew what He was doing all the time.

Now, a few years later, I'm still serving Him in different ministries and helping my love, who is doing nationwide men's ministries.

Without God and my love's support, I wouldn't have made it. God keeps putting these movies in front of me, like *Heaven is for Real*. I have breakdown cries when they show that bright light, because I saw it in my experience. God gave me the assurance that nothing I have done is too big or bad. He has forgiven me. He has set me free to be a light to others, showing them the life that God gives after you accept Him into your life.

My love and I have found the true happiness that comes through Jesus. God has filled that empty spot from not having my own kids. He filled the void with many families adopting me into their lives, sharing their babies with me and my sweetheart.

Maybe my life is a tale like Mary Poppins after all. I am certainly assured of a happy ending.

Vickie Lubbock is Gigi to her kids, "G" as in game. She is a professional nanny who has nannied for doctors, lawyers, senators, movie stars, nurses, engineers, and realtors. She is a minister's wife who loves to do ministry with her sweetheart. She loves to sing and is minister in music to the elderly at a nursing rehab. She also has a ministry worldwide on Facebook, where she shares her testimonies and witnesses to all about God's love, grace, and forgiveness. Her fun hobby is going to Goodwill, picking out beautiful outfits for her date nights and other occasions, then putting pictures on Facebook to show how classy you can dress inexpensively.

Thoughts to Ponder

from Just like Mary Poppins

1. God is always ready to forgive.

2. God alone can fill the void in our life.

3. For believers, there should be no fear of death.

From what do you need to be set free?

He has anointed me to proclaim good news to the poor. . . . to proclaim freedom for the prisoners. — Luke 4:18

Misdiagnosed

by Tabitha Ferguson

Several years ago, I sat in jail, completely broken. I felt like I was losing my mind. I was a failure and a loser, because I couldn't function in society. I couldn't hold a steady job. I wasn't a stable mother to my twin boys, and I was a high school dropout who had lost her identity. I was trapped in lies and negative thoughts that tormented me. I didn't know how to cope, and learned at a very young age to medicate my emotions instead of addressing my wounded soul.

Society can make us believe we're mentally ill, because people only see the symptoms of our emotional and mental struggles. They don't thoroughly assess our lives or understand how traumatic events affect our bodies. The sad part about the things I endured was being surrounded by people who proclaimed Jesus Christ as their Savior, yet they ran around chasing the ninety-nine instead of reaching out to the one who was lost.

Many pushed the idea of salvation and told me as a little girl, if I didn't believe in Jesus, then I'd burn in Hell for an eternity. So I accepted Jesus into my heart. Since they didn't invest in my life beyond the invitation and baptism, I was living an *internal* hell. Looking back, I know that wasn't the way to lead someone to Christ. I was led by fear. As a ten-year-old who already struggled with fear, anxiety, and depression, that message traumatized me and left wounds so deep I couldn't cope with life.

Before I learned my alphabet or could speak complete sentences, sexual perversion invaded my innocence. I also experienced high levels of stress through my mother, who blamed everything on her diagnosis of schizophrenia and was in and out of mental institutions. I didn't know what self-care was, because my traumatic events were minimized by everyone around me. While I took care of a mom who was supposed to love and nurture me, I faced emotional battles with distorted thoughts that I didn't know how to deal with alone. The seeds of not being loved or valued—not feeling good enough—took deep root in my mind and continued to grow for many years. I became lost in addictions and street life. Since everyone around me trivialized the burdens I carried and didn't feel my deep sorrow, I naturally put on a fake smile and moved on without processing.

As I got older, I grew colder toward humanity, including my mom. I lost interest in school and no longer cared about academic work. When I went to school, I lacked social skills, because of life at home and on the streets. To deal with my emotions and behavior and because my mind was stressed, they placed me in special education. I was labeled with mental illnesses that I didn't have and was loaded up on psychiatric medications. I was set up to fail. Bullying from my peers didn't help. I faced a broken home life and dysfunction in the classroom. I never felt safe.

I was eleven years old when I started smoking cigarettes and began to have eating disorders. When I looked at myself in the mirror, I was disgusted with what I saw and was haunted with negative thoughts about myself. Since my classmates called me names daily, I was convinced that I looked like a horse, with my skinny legs and a big midsection. I saw myself as fat and ugly, because that's what my mother often said. She introduced me to the bar life when I was twelve, exposing me to the lifestyle that would entrap me for years down the road.

I didn't shop in the girl's section, because I felt unworthy to dress like a lady. Instead, I browsed the men's section and wouldn't wear anything that showed my body shape. I looked at magazines to teach myself how to apply makeup, but I still didn't believe I was anything more than a sex object, since I had been exposed to sexual perversion when I was two. In middle school and high school, boys didn't ask me out. I compared myself as someone inferior to the girls who did have the boyfriends, girly clothes, and jewelry.

At fourteen, I could not function in the classroom anymore, so the school kicked me out and placed me in a school overseen by the juvenile system. We had to wear jumpsuits like criminals and faced drill instructors who yelled and cursed at us during physical training. I was losing myself even more and became trapped in lies that sunk deep into my soul. With chronic fear and heartache, I wanted to die.

160

As I declined mentally and emotionally, my behavior got worse, with rages almost daily. My mom had to call the cops on me, because I didn't know how to function at home. My juvenile probation officer told me I was on my way to a prison for youth if I didn't straighten up, but I honestly didn't know how. Since I couldn't function at home, juvenile probation decided to move me to a treatment facility instead of the prison for youth. The first home was another unsafe environment, with girls who had also come from dysfunctional backgrounds. They mistreated me the entire time I was there. I don't remember much about the next home. At that point, as a coping mechanism, I had learned to disassociate and separate myself from the constant trauma. I still can't remember many of my experiences there.

When I was about to turn seventeen, juvenile probation decided to move me in with my grandpa, which seemed like the best idea since it was a stable home life. Everything was good at first. I was happy to be back in my hometown. I thought I was on the road to recovery until I started my junior year in a Christian private school. My experiences there were no different, and I was bullied by most of my peers. The way they treated me broke my spirit even more. I turned my back on God and went to the streets with others who were running from their broken homes. I began smoking marijuana, which led me to drink alcohol and do the harder drugs such as cocaine, methamphetamines, and narcotic pain pills. Since I didn't know how to cope, I turned to anything that would numb my emotions and negative thoughts. You might think getting pregnant with twin boys would slow me down and change my behavior, but it didn't. I didn't know how to function in a healthy way. After they were born, I continued to run the streets.

I had frequent mental breakdowns, repeating the same cycle I watched my mother go through with mental hospitals. I woke up in ICU a few times, because I had attempted suicide and failed. My angry outbursts were uncontrollable, like a wild lion in a cage.

At twenty-four, I sat in jail without hope. I cried out to God in anger, because I couldn't take the pain anymore. I hated the mistreatment by people who proclaimed Christianity. As I sat in jail, loaded up on a high psychiatric tranquilizer, I kept writing one phrase as the tears rolled down my cheeks: *The truth will set you free.* I didn't understand what the words meant, but I held on to them as if they were my only hope. That sentence was an anchor in one of the most hopeless times in my life. I was tired of not being understood or valued. I was tired of being made fun of by people who said I was crazy. I was tired of the street life that I couldn't break free from. I was tired of the mental breakdowns. I was tired of waking up in ICU from failed suicide attempts.

I was tired, and God knew I was tired. He heard my desperate cry for help as I pleaded with Him to either take me or take the pain away. He rescued me—what the church had failed to do when I cried out for help.

When I got out of jail, I was facing several charges and felt completely worthless. I went back to twelve-step meetings even though I cringed on the inside when they kept telling me I had a disease that caused my addictions. During my time there, a guy kept giving me these self-help books by an evangelist named Joyce Meyer. I was apprehensive at first, because I had started her book *Me and My Big Mouth* before jail and felt even more hopeless. The book was way above my spiritual maturity level. I needed milk, not meat. However, her *Battlefield of the Mind* sustained me as I began a journey into new hope. I slowly reintegrated and functioned in society because of what I learned through her sermons online and on television. She was different from other church people I had encountered. She talked about the abuse with her dad and mom. For the first time in my life, I felt connected with someone who understood me.

I began to walk in a relationship with Jesus, something I was never taught when growing up. I saw some changes. A year later, I was reading the book of John when God shared a deep revelation, which took me to a whole new level with Him. Jesus said, "If you hold to my teaching, you are really my disciples. Then you will know the truth, and the truth will set you free" (John 8:31-32).

The truth will set you free.

I immediately made a connection with the phrase I had kept

writing in jail. Then I had no doubt that God and Christianity were real.

After a few years in early recovery and learning how to function in society, I decided to look into my past by pulling records, hoping to find closure. To my surprise, I found almost two thousand documents from our local Child Protective Services (CPS), documenting my cries for help for eight years. Five of the eight years, CPS investigated. Their local clinician documented that I was in an unsafe environment that interfered with my overall functioning. At ten years old, I was diagnosed with anxiety, depression, and body dysmorphia—a mental disorder characterized by the obsessive idea that one's own body part or appearance is severely flawed. Instead of someone in authority looking into my mental distresses, I was heavily medicated with psychiatric drugs. As I got older, the mental illness labels stacked against me, and I got lost in even more false identities. I later discovered that I had symptoms of Post-Traumatic Stress Disorder (PTSD) but was not diagnosed until my early thirties. They documented that when I was twenty-one years old I was on a seventh-grade level emotionally, mentally, and intellectually.

All the documents and paper trails explained why I couldn't function in society and fell into addictions and street life. I learned that trauma is paralleled to traumatic brain injury, which interfered with my natural development. I saw why I couldn't control my anger and rage. I didn't know how to self-regulate, because I was never taught how to cope in a healthy way. Instead, I was taught how to manage using psych medications to cover up the internal damage from the trauma. Our nervous systems get caught when we don't process traumatic events, which explained why I had panic attacks and suffered from anxiety.

My season in jail was over eleven years ago, and it's been quite a journey. I've had to clean up a ton of messes over the years as I've lived every stage of grief, unmedicated. I've had to grieve my losses and redefine what was taken from me. By grace I've been given another chance at life. I continue a journey of healing and restoration while I stand in the gap for those who need a voice. This is my "why" when I wake up every day and face people in our system. I help others clean up the messes that took me over a decade to clean up. I sit on local and statewide committees with Texas Systems of Care as I share openly and publicly about the damage one goes through without proper intervention.

PTSD is one of the most misdiagnosed brain disorders that can be healed and restored with the right counselor, an intimate relationship with the One Who created us, and supportive friends and family. Not many people understand our healing process, so I am currently writing my first book as I share in detail what it's like living through and coming out of a traumatic background.

If someone in authority would have properly responded to my cries for help, I believe I would have followed a much better path. Because of my healing and restoration, I have gained custody of my twin boys. They are doing well, considering everything they watched me go through.

There are five stages in grief. When we heal from trauma, we go through the same emotions as someone losing a loved one, because we are grieving the loss of never having a normal childhood. People in mental health need to understand trauma and grief instead of labeling someone with a mental illness. I had a list of diagnoses that I didn't have, such as bipolar, personality disorder, abnormal brain cells that caused blackout rages, and anxiety and depression disorder. Every one of these false diagnoses took years to break free from—lies spoken over me that something was wrong. Because nobody took the time to let me process and heal my mind and soul from the trauma, I lived with the false burdens of shame and guilt.

Nobody can ever give me back what I lost growing up, but I share openly and publicly so I can help others understand the misunderstood. I do not want others to have to clean as many messes as I've had to clean up over the years. God didn't create personality disorders, bipolar disorder, abnormal brain cells that cause rages, anxiety, and depression disorders. He created good, and He is faithful. He said throughout His Word that He heals the brokenhearted. He binds up our wounds and restores our souls. It's up to us as survivors to redefine what the enemy meant for harm.

Tabitha Ferguson *was born and raised in Central Texas. She is a single mom of twin boys. She recently graduated from Tarleton State University as a first-time college graduate in her family. She majored in business and minored in mental health. She enjoys spending time hiking, biking, swimming, gardening, and exploring state parks and trails. Tabitha uses her life experiences from a traumatic past to raise awareness about mental health and addictions. She is writing her first book and blogs about her journey. Her blogs can be found at* **RedeemedLoved1.wordpress.com.**

Thoughts to Ponder
from Misdiagnosed

1. God wants to restore us both emotionally and spiritually.

2. The lies of the past can be undone through faith in Jesus Christ.

3. We can help others heal because of our own healing.

How have you been misunderstood?

To the Jews who had believed him, Jesus said, "If you hold to my teaching, you are really my disciples. Then you will know the truth, and the truth will set you free." — John 8:31–32

Shattered Glass
by Estella Lyon Davis

Do you enjoy looking out the window in your home? Do you like stained glass windows? Those are not as transparent, only proving that not all windows allow us to see clearly. Windows can also be cracked, scratched, and shattered—a lot like the windows of our lives.

When one window was shattered, my life ceased to be as I had known it. Two police officers rang our doorbell in the middle of the night. They were there to tell me and my husband that our eighteen-year-old son, Jake, had died in an automobile accident. I asked my husband to tell me I was dreaming. The officer said, "This is not a dream ma'am. Your son is dead."

It took only two phone calls to find out where Jake had been. When I told a mother that Jake had died from an automobile accident, she screamed in agony and told me everything. She had allowed underage kids to drink alcohol and smoke weed at her house, thinking it was a safe place. Her oldest son bought wine, and Jake consumed the whole bottle. They encouraged Jake to stay the night, but he wanted to come home, since he was starting a new job the next day. After agreeing to stay, he went outside to smoke a cigarette. A few seconds later, the mother saw the taillights of his car as he drove away. I told her I forgave her and her son, and I hoped she would never let underage kids drink at her house again. I thought, *How could people live with themselves, knowing they had a part in someone else's death?*

I felt pain I never knew was possible. Now I know what other parents feel when they lose a child. I thought, *What if I live another twenty to thirty years? I can't live that long without Jake.* Life went on for others, but life stood still for me.

There was another window I could not see through clearly. My other son, Randy, was in a rehab center. We knew he had been drinking and smoking weed and were trying to get him help. Two weeks after Jake died, I decided I would not lose this son to substance abuse. I gave Randy the choice to either check into a rehab center or to live at the Salvation Army. He chose to get help. After being there a few months, he was diagnosed with Post Traumatic Stress Disorder (PTSD) from the death of his father four years earlier. Randy had been self-medicating to dull the pain. After his diagnosis, we realized that Jake might have had the same problem.

The boys' dad died from a massive heart attack while they were spending the weekend with him. He died in Jake's arms while Randy was frantically looking out the window for the ambulance. Jake said their dad died a painful death. That experience was devastating for my boys. I took them to grief counseling for a while, but they fought me on it.

Randy had been hurting from losing his dad, and now he was also grieving for his brother. I wished I could bear his pain, but that was not possible.

The pain became too much for me to bear. I felt as if I had lost both boys. All my dreams for them were shattered. I could not see past the pain. I felt alone, and I didn't want to live. I thought about suicide and how I could end it all.

Another window was difficult to look through. Tom, my second husband of twenty-two years, died suddenly from legionnaires' disease. Losing him was hard for me, emotionally and physically. I had to run our business, attend to house repairs, and adjust to life without my loving husband. But the actions of my stepson and his wife made my grief unbearable. I came to see their true colors after learning that they had been manipulating the financials of a business we had together. And then they tried to turn my grandkids away from me with lies. I was deeply hurt and shocked. The mere thought of losing my grandkids was devastating.

One window opened for me recently when I posted #metoo on Facebook. For forty-five years, I had carried the guilt and shame of being raped, my first sexual experience. I was fifteen, and my rapist was twenty. His name has left me, but I can still clearly see his face. As an adult, I attempted to look into the window of that house, but I always turned away quickly, telling myself how stupid I was for putting myself in that situation.

I sneaked out of the house and went with two of my friends to a party. People knew when I was being raped, but no one came to my rescue. After we got back home, my girlfriend told me that her boyfriend was mad at his friend for what he did to me. My friends were more excited to have gone to the party than being upset about what happened to me. I was hurting and confused, but I didn't let my feelings show. I had never even been kissed before. I never told my parents, and thankfully we moved within a year to another school.

In the fall of 2015, a college student was arrested and put on trial for raping a female student. I wondered if what had happened to me would be considered rape today. I could not get beyond that thought and again turned away from that window. But in May 2016, the words "it was rape" was magnified in my head. The message was not audible, but it took my breath away. The thing that happened to me now had a name. I told myself, *Of course, it was rape. Why would I think any differently? Was this the mindset of a fifteen-year-old?* With that knowledge came the feeling of being violated.

Looking back, I now see more clearly the windows of opportunity that came from these terrible experiences. I learned who I was in Christ, that He loves me, and that He has a purpose for me.

When I lost my son, I experienced a depth of love from Christ that was beyond words, and I wanted everyone to know there was more to Jesus than most realize.

My mother-in-law once told me, "You know who you are."

I asked her, "What do you mean?"

"You know who you are in your faith, and you live it." She said it was very rare.

I said, "Well, I try." My deep, deep love of Christ was my gain from the loss of my son, and I would not change losing my son if it meant losing what I have in Christ.

After Jake's death, the Lord gave me passion for life. My love for Jake was extended in my love for the Lord and my love for others. Jake's high school let his friends leave school when they received the news of his death. We suddenly had around forty kids at our house. I loved on those kids, tried to comfort them, and shared Jesus with them. Through the Lord's strength, I was able to speak at Jake's funeral. Over 150 kids were there. Afterward, I stood at the front and handed each one a Gideon Bible. Many of them have told me they gave their life to Christ that day. Later, the school principal asked me to speak to their students. That began my new path in life.

I started speaking to the youth at middle schools, high schools, and churches. I showed pictures of Jake's mangled car. I wanted everyone to know what happened to him and that it could happen to them. I also shared my faith. Afterward, these kids were so eager to tell me about a family member or friend who had substance abuse issues. Some just wanted to give me a hug. One girl said, "Thank you for sharing Jake's story." She had planned to kill herself that day. She didn't want her family to hurt like I was hurting. I hugged her and didn't want to let go. Everything she wore was black. She was involved in Wicca and was addicted to cocaine. We became very close, and I mentored her for three years. She is a success story, loving the Lord, free of drugs, and married.

One Sunday, Jake's friend and a buddy came to our church. Some of the kids had told us Jake was not around this friend as much, as he was using heroin. We were so happy to see both of them. They were obviously high on drugs. As our pastor preached his sermon, I just prayed over those boys. I could tell they were touched by God. After the sermon, they went down front and professed Christ as their Savior. Our preacher arranged for them to come back for counseling, but they never did. Afterward, the boys joined us for lunch. They cried their hearts out and thanked us for loving them as they were, being addicts and all.

A couple of months later, I got news that the boy we didn't personally know had died from an overdose. He had been trying to get clean. His father was taking him to a rehab center a distance away. They stayed in a hotel the night before he was to be admitted, when he shot up one last time. I asked my preacher to go to the viewing and share their son's visit from that Sunday. That knowledge would be a gift, something they would cling to during their darkest days. The parents said their son accepted Christ as a young boy, but they were so grateful to know he had reached out to the Lord before his death. Romans 6:23 says, "For the wages of sin is death, but the gift of God is eternal life in Christ Jesus our Lord." Even if I only influenced one life, my son's life lives on. It is worth his death to bring someone to life in Christ.

Before my husband died, we joined local businesses and individuals in East Texas to build a skate park in Malakoff, in memory of our son. Jake was an avid skater. It is a drug and alcohol awareness park. We started a skate ministry with competitions and Bible studies. Many kids have come to know the Lord through this ministry.

For twelve years, I have led a women's grief support group.

If it were not for the death of my son, these ministries wouldn't be in existence today. Seeing God's hand in my life and in the life of others helps me tremendously. Jeremiah 29:11 says, "'I know the plans I have for you,' declares the Lord, 'plans to prosper you and not to harm you, plans to give you hope and a future.'"

As I look out the window now, I see a future with hope. Instead of suicidal thoughts, I experience the joy of the Lord.

Having suicidal thoughts really scared me. I reached out to my pastor for spiritual help and my doctor for medical help. I took depression medicine for six months and began praying in faith and thanksgiving for the day my son, Randy, would have freedom from self-medicating. That day came. Praise God! Romans 8:18 assures us that our "present sufferings are not worth comparing with the glory that will be revealed in us."

I continually gave Randy to God and let God take over. He brought Randy through that most difficult time. I am so proud of his accomplishments. Today he is living in Dallas and works as a licensed pet groomer. He loves his job, and not too many can say that.

While trying to repair the window to my business, I realized that only God could sever my working relationship with my stepson and his wife. His wife and I had come to an agreement. I would sell them my shares, but then she changed her mind. A few weeks later, I read Psalm 86:17: "Give me a sign of your goodness, that my enemies may see it and be put to shame, for you, Lord, have helped me and comforted me." I wrote the words on a note card, with my daughter-in-law's name in place of "enemies." I sat there and asked, *Is she really my enemy?*" And I thought, *Yes*. No one but an enemy would send me hateful and lying emails and copy to my grandkids. That evening, a business associate of hers called me. She had an instinct that she was not hearing the truth and wanted to hear my side of the story. Within twenty-four hours, she called me again and said, "I think I can shame her into following through with the agreement," and that is what she did. There is power in praying God's Word.

It was a huge financial loss for me. I did not give my stepson and his wife the same treatment as I was given. I turned the other cheek. They divorced a year later. Their family has been torn apart. My stepson and I no longer have a relationship, but we are cordial. One grandson does not communicate with me. I have tried phoning and texting, but to no avail. I'm trusting Exodus 14:14: "The Lord will fight for you; you need only to be still." His brother and sister love me dearly and are a part of my life. Their love is priceless to me.

"Facing myself" was my window to clearly reach freedom. When I let go, Christ was right there with me. He took away the guilt and shame from my rape and eventually from feeling violated.

Having Jesus by your side does not mean life will be easy. We must work through certain emotions to heal. My pastor's wife mentored me for a while, and I started journaling. I began telling my family, friends, and female business associates about my rape. Philippians 4:13 promises, "I can do all this through him who gives me strength." His driving power led me to share. From those I told, nine out of twelve had been sexually abused or raped. Some were like me and had never told anyone. These women would now have a measure of freedom by sharing their story with me.

The day before I shared with one of my friends, she had thought about what happened to her as a little girl. She wondered how her life would have been different if that had not happened, and she wondered if it was her fault. Hearing my story was confirmation from the Lord that it was not her fault. She had freedom from the guilt and shame.

Romans 8:28 tells us that God works good out of the bad in our lives. "And we know that in all things God works for the good of those who love him, who have been called according to his purpose." Behind the window I could never look into, God is using the devastation to give me a new desire in my heart. I yearn to reach out to women who have been sexually violated. What happened to me does not define me, nor does it define you if you are a victim.

My comfort comes from feeling God's love. Nothing can change that. He is my strength and comfort. He is putting the pieces of shattered glass back together.

Answered prayer gave me a window filled with sunshine. I never thought I would marry again. I just thought I would travel with my sister. But after two years, I started to think it would be nice to have a man in my life. That thought really surprised me. I made a list of important characteristics I wanted in a man. My pastor's wife told me to pick out three to four that were most important. I didn't tell her I already had well over a dozen, so I got the list down to eight.

I wanted a man who loved God and was already attending church. I didn't want to change him, and church was an important part of my life. I wanted a man with integrity, who was giving of himself, a giver monetarily to others, who was loving and attentive—a non-drinker. I didn't want drinking to ever be an issue.

I decided to ask God for a widower after meeting a divorcee online who said I should not talk about my husband. He was giving me tidbits of advice on dating. By the way, after meeting the divorcee, I took myself off that dating site. I stopped looking for a man and started trusting God and His timing.

I prayed over this man for two years. I prayed the Lord would watch over him and help him overcome any struggles in life. I asked for his faith and love for the Lord to be strengthened. I continuously thanked the Lord for the day that we would meet.

A year earlier, David had lost his wife, one of my sister's best friends. For fifteen years, we both had heard stories about each other and our spouses. On the day we met, David was about to post his profile on a dating site, but God had other plans. I call David my dream man, because he is all the things on my list and much more. People tell us they see the love in us. I believe it's because David and I share a love inspired by God, and we give God the glory. John 15:7 says, "If you remain in me and my words remain in you, ask whatever you wish, and it will be done for you."

I have a stained glass window in my home. You can see God's Word from Matthew 28:20 in the window, and it says, "I am with you always." This is clearly a visual declaration that God's Spirit is always with us. But more importantly, it is truth for those who have opened the windows of their hearts to Jesus.

Estella Lyon Davis is purpose driven for Christ and has a heart for those who hurt. She has taught women's grief classes for the last twelve years and is involved in her church. Estella has shared the story of her son's life and his death from DUI. She has spoken to many youth at schools and churches. She is blessed beyond measure in her new marriage to David, an answer to prayer. In her free time, she enjoys her rose garden, traveling, jigsaw puzzles, Christian concerts, and visiting her grandkids. She can be reached at EstellaLyon@gmail.com.

Thoughts to Ponder
from Shattered Glass

1. When the windows of our lives shatter, God can put the pieces back together.

2. God can heal the deepest of emotional pain and violation.

3. The Lord hears the desires of our heart.

What windows need to be repaired in your life?

I can do all this through him who gives me strength. — Philippians 4:13

Lost and Found
by Gaye Ganter

The captain of a ship was sailing on a pitch-black night. He noticed a bright light directly in front of him and knew his ship was on a collision course with the light, so he sent an urgent radio message demanding that the vessel change its course ten degrees east.

A few seconds later, a message came in return. "Cannot do it. Change *your* course ten degrees west."

Angry, the captain voiced a cryptic message. "I'm a Navy Captain. I demand you change your course."

The message back said, "I'm a Seaman Second Class. Cannot do it. Change your course."

Now furious, the captain gave his final warning: "I'm a battleship, and I'm not changing my course."

The seaman curtly replied, "I'm a lighthouse. It's your choice, sir."

Whenever I hear this story, I'm reminded of our eternity and our choice for either Heaven or Hell. I was like that battleship captain, doing it my way, totally unaware that I was heading straight to Hell.

ଓ • ଆ

When I was born, my parents were forty-three years old. I have two older brothers. We're all exactly twelve years apart. I was born on my oldest brother's twenty-fourth birthday. My mom always said she was going to write a book, but she had two titles to choose from: *Thirty-Six Years in the PTA* or *Three Only Children*. I was an accident, but I was the bonus baby—a girl.

My oldest brother was married with a family. My next brother was twelve when I was born. Tough age. I can imagine how difficult it must have been to no longer be in the spotlight, the center of attention. My brother turned to drugs to satisfy his need. He was very violent. He would come home raging at my parents, kicking doors and walls. I was scared to death of him, and I felt like he was killing my parents. I knew I had to be perfectly opposite for them. When I was in the second grade and both brothers had moved out of the house, my parents

176

placed me in a private Christian school. They believed in God and wanted the same for me. I learned a lot about Jesus at home and at school and became a Christian.

In the sixth grade, we moved across town, and I enrolled in public school. I had a great life. My grandmother lived with us, and I had her undivided attention. I was daddy's girl, and my mom was my strength. However, at age fifteen, a guy came to my school who was very good-looking. He was a bad boy. I knew it, but I wanted his attention. I never knew how old he was, just that he was older than me. I was a cheerleader when he finally asked me out, during basketball season. I cheered at a game and met him afterward. We went to the liquor store, and I drank. I remember going to his apartment. Then I woke up in the emergency room. I have never recovered memories of that fateful night.

I found out later that I made it home from the "date." When I got into bed with my grandmother, she asked, "How was the date?" I didn't answer, so she turned on the light. My eyes were rolled back in my head, so they rushed me to the hospital. The evidence from my clothes said I had been date-raped.

I kept thinking, *It's my fault. I should've been in control. It's not his fault.* My mom told me I could never see him again. And that "incident" was never spoken about again.

A week later, I was called into the school office and was told to phone my mom. She said I needed to go straight to the hospital. My blood work from that night revealed very high blood sugars, but the hospital had lost the report. I was diagnosed with juvenile diabetes (Type 1). It took a while for me to realize the "incident" was a blessing in disguise. If left untreated, I could have ended up in ketoacidosis, gone into a coma, and died.

I learned the hard way that love cannot be forced. Although I straightened up my act on the outside, I grew farther away from God. As a girl, I did learn a Bible story from Matthew 18:12–14: "If a man owns a hundred sheep, and one of them wanders away, will he not leave the ninety-nine on the hills and go to look for the one that wandered off? And if he finds it, truly I tell you, he is happier about that one sheep than about the ninety-nine that did not wander off. In the same way your Father in

Heaven is not willing that any of these little ones should perish."

I learned that Jesus is our Shepherd, and we are His sheep. He is *constantly* looking for us, but God gives us a choice to choose Him—no forced love.

Like a lost sheep, I wandered off. I could see the flock, but I got distracted by life and my own selfish concerns. I knew Jesus was there, but I wanted to do things my way. I knew what was right, but I chose the wrong—a lot. As Dr. Phil would say, "How's that working out for ya?"

One day at church, a woman came up to me and said, "Gaye, I feel like God wants me to tell you that you are a sheep." She didn't know what that meant, just that she needed to share. I had forgotten the Bible story from so long ago and had no idea where her words could've come from. I was in denial.

∞ • ∞

While running with her college soccer team, my daughter found Bear, a stray dog, in a cemetery in Arkansas. Bear became my DAD (Diabetes Alert Dog). People pay thousands of dollars for this service, but Bear was gifted. She would wake my husband if my blood sugars went low, even in the middle of the night. She was a God-send in my life.

God used our dog, a Bible study, and my mom to bring me back to Him. My husband and I took a weekend getaway with friends. We had three dogs, so we planned for our kids to take care of two of them at our house. However, my husband insisted that Bear stay with my husband's parents. At 6:00 Sunday morning, my husband and I were out on the porch, drinking coffee and admiring the beautiful scenery. Then it occurred to me that there was only one thing missing: the dogs. At that second, my husband's cell phone rang. It couldn't be good news.

His dad told him Bear was missing. She had gotten out the day before. Ten adults looked for Bear the whole day. I wanted to go home immediately, but I didn't have our car. The next few hours were gut-wrenching. I finally asked our friends if we could go home, because we had to find Bear.

We went straight to the place she was last seen and scoured the streets, calling her name and searching to well past dark.

- I made posters and signs with my cell number on them.
- I called and visited dog shelters, veterinarian offices, animal hospitals, and was in constant communication with animal control in seven-plus cities.
- I used Facebook, Craigslist, and email.
- I even hired a pet detective, another story for another time.

When we weren't at work, we were desperately searching for Bear. About a week in, I asked my husband, "How are we gonna know when to stop looking?" That's when it hit me. *This is how God feels when I wander away from Him.* It was just like the Bible story I had heard so long ago. He loves each of us dearly, every moment of every day. He's got the signs out. He's imploring help from "pet detectives"—helpers, preachers, evangelists, newscasters, and our friends. He uses radio, TV, and billboards. God is very creative. There are messages all around us, but like Bear, we are consumed with ourselves, and we are unaware of the methods God is using to bring us to Him.

When I was in my thirties, I attended a Bible study. One of the questions was, "Who is your hero? Who do you go to for advice, direction, or guidance?" My answer was my grandmother, my dad, and my mom. I adored these three people. They were my foundation. Then I turned the page, and the Bible study asked, "How about God as your hero?" Hmm. That had never entered my mind.

When I was twenty years of age, my grandmother died.

At thirty, my dad died.

At forty, my mom fell and broke her hip.

All my human heroes were falling one-by-one.

Mom had surgery, which according to the doctor went well, but days went by, and she didn't wake up from the anesthesia. Why was this happening? I went by myself to the hospital chapel, pulled down the kneeler, and took a Bible in my hands. "God," I said, "what is going on here?" I opened the Bible, and my eyes fell on John 14:1-4: "Do not let your hearts be troubled. You believe in God; believe also in me. My Father's house has many rooms; if that were not so, would I have told you that I am going there to prepare a place for you? And if I go and prepare a place for you, I will come back and take you to be with me that you also may be where I am. You know the way to the place where I am going."

I had peace. I told my mom goodbye and that I would be fine. She took her final breath. I didn't physically see Jesus that morning, but I felt like God had reached down His hand and whispered, "Now let Me be your hero and guide you."

God definitely got my attention. I was that sheep. I told God how sorry I was for not taking Him seriously, for wandering away from Him, and hurting Him so many times.

Are you wondering what happened to Bear? She was out there wandering—trying to do things her way when she finally realized she needed help. I believe that what started out as an adventure ended up a quest for life. She was hot, tired, thirsty, hungry, and worn out. She finally gave in and surrendered. She approached a house and asked for help. It was two weeks and two days later—after the dog days of summer—that my phone rang and someone said, "I think I found your dog."

God had allowed me to experience a small glimpse of what He feels.

My grandmother and I used to read poems together. The one about the poor little black sheep never impacted me until now. A little black sheep had strayed, lost in the wind and rain until the shepherd left the ninety-nine that were safe and found the one that was lost. He held the sheep close, and that little sheep is me.

Now, I'm plugged in—I *love* church. I even pay attention. I love Bible studies and learning about God—I love God! I make a concerted effort to read my Bible daily and talk with God throughout the day. We are growing our relationship. I can now say, "The Lord *is my* Shepherd."

Gaye Ganter is a native of Dallas. She dated Mark, her high school sweetheart, for five years, and they were married on the anniversary of their first date. She has two children, Nikki and Zak. She always enjoys her dogs and grand dogs, and it is not uncommon for her to host "Camp Grandma," where all five grand dogs visit. She worked at and sold Pampered Chef for ten years and has worked for Starbucks for the last sixteen years. In her spare time, she loves to read and Bible doodle.

Thoughts to Ponder
from Lost and Found

1. Sometimes we must change our course to avoid a collision.

2. The one lost sheep is the first one God goes after.

3. God wants to be our hero.

> ## *How has God brought you back to Him?*

We all, like sheep, have gone astray, each of us has turned to our own way; and the Lord has laid on him the iniquity of us all. — Isaiah 53:6

God Is Calling

by Gina Morrison

Think back to your early years. Do you remember those years before you became a Christian? Can you pinpoint moments in your history where you knew God was calling you, but you couldn't see past the worldly struggles to realize the answer was in front of you?

When I look at my life, I see moments where God was with me. He was there during my struggles and my pain, calling me to Him. He was with me as I witnessed my mother being physically and emotionally abused. He was near when, as a four-year-old latchkey child, I tried to care for myself until my mother got home from work. As I cried out to Him, He was with me through unspeakable pain and heartache, even though I didn't fully believe in Him.

My mother was a child of the sixties and seventies, a runaway teen, in and out of foster care. She dated a string of abusive men and drank to excess. She was insecure, emotionally fragile, and a lost soul, continuously seeking the next man to fill the loneliness deep inside. Her faults were many, but by the age of nineteen, she became a mom—my mom. The two of us depended on each other to make it in this world.

We lived in a little town in northern California, next to the redwood forests with trees so big that a two-lane highway could fit through the tree trunk. We moved from place to place in that area until I was eight-years-old. One afternoon, she picked me up early from school in her silver 1980 Honda Accord. The hatchback was packed to the top with whatever she could fit in. As I moved closer to the car, my stomach started to knot up. Something was wrong. She had never picked me up early before.

As I opened the door, I saw bruises on her face, her arms, and her hands. She had been in and out of bad relationships where I witnessed verbal and physical abuse. One time, she was knocked down a small hill off the side of a highway, and she rolled into a nearby ditch. That memory still stings. I lived with fear that someday one of these men would kill her, and I would be left with no one. Many nights, I prayed to an anonymous god up in the sky, asking him to save my mom. I listened to her and her boyfriend in the next room yelling and hitting each other. Eventually, there was just the sound of her crying quietly. I didn't know if God existed, but I felt deep inside that He might. I sat on my bed, hot tears streaming down my cheeks, praying that this higher power would miraculously make these men disappear—or that my mother might gain the strength one day to leave. On this school-day afternoon, my prayers had finally been answered. We were packed and ready to go. A combination of sadness and immense relief coursed through my body, with an unspoken sense that we would be okay.

We moved down the California coast and landed in San Diego for a year, living with my mom's childhood foster family for a brief period. After that, we floated from friend to friend until the generosity eventually ran out. My mother decided we should head east to Florida, where my grandparents lived. Knowing our little Honda wasn't going to make the journey, she bought two one-way bus tickets.

We loaded everything we could fit into two large suitcases and boarded the Greyhound bus. I sat on the dingy, poorly padded seats and gazed at the scenery through Arizona, New Mexico, and beyond. As we rode through miles of desert sand, crossed deep canyons, and saw a kaleidoscope of shapes and colors, I pressed my head against the window and closed my eyes.

I dreamed of peaceful nights and having my own bedroom. I imagined being reunited with my grandparents. They were the safe place I relied on so often during my early years in California. When they moved away, I felt abandoned. My grandfather, especially, had met the need that a little girl without a father has. He was pure magic in my eyes, and I was his first grandchild—the apple of his eye.

He spent countless hours teaching me about drawing and painting. I saw the wonder of nature as we walked through the Redwoods and peered above, standing in awe of the towering treetops. He taught me the pure joy of plucking a honeysuckle flower from its bush and extracting the sweet nectar, which kept me hydrated on warm summer afternoons. I longed for more moments like that. After a few days, we finally made it to

Florida. As the bus pulled into the station, I saw my grandparents waiting to greet us. I had mixed feelings of nervousness, happiness, and hope.

When hope comes from people, trouble often follows. People are fallible, and they can fail you. As a foundation, they never provide real stability. As Matthew 7 says, when you build your foundation on sand, the winds and the rain will surely make the house fall. Without God, life's foundation is unstable sand. I thought our move to Florida would be the answer to our problems, but my twenty-nine-year-old mother repeated her old pattern of binge drinking, poor relationships with men, and using me as an emotional security blanket.

A year later, we were still living with my grandparents. Their neighborhood was a child's dream—a long street with mobile homes, houses, and a little church that held about five hundred people. A small army of children lived on this street. If we weren't at school, we were outside playing together, with youthful imaginations.

I loved being with my grandparents. I felt safe, and those knots that had lived in my stomach for so many years finally loosened. But I could tell that my grandparent's patience with our home invasion was growing thin.

My mom was working and saving up to pay off her car and get our own apartment. She was eager to reclaim her independence. My grandparents had a way of letting her know when they disapproved of her life choices, and as a full-grown adult, their judgments unnerved her. The latest string of bad choices had led to another pregnancy, with a man who didn't want the responsibilities of fatherhood. News of the baby did not receive the reaction she was hoping for and proved to be a catalyst for more fights with my grandparents. Our days were numbered, as they informed her it was time to leave their home. Anxiety welled up inside me and that draw to God once again began to stir.

But who was God?

I was ten years old and had probably seen enough on television to know something about Jesus. I thought the little church at the end of the road might have the answer to what I was looking for. I had never been to church before. What was it

184

going to be like? Would people ask me questions and judge me because I have never read the Bible? Most important to an insecure little girl, I asked, *What do you even wear to church?* I put on what I considered dress-up clothes. Keep in mind, I was a child of the eighties and nineties. I wore tight acid-wash jeans with colorful splashes of paint sprinkled haphazardly, a kitty kat shirt that sat at the waist, and grey high heels borrowed from my mom. I'm not sure they fit me. And yes, that morning my family let me leave the house and walk to church in a clothing atrocity.

I'd like to tell you I was wrong to fear judgment from church, but my experience that Sunday morning was mostly what I expected. The greeters directed me toward Sunday school, where all the kids were gathering. As I walked in, I saw them forming a seated circle. Each child was dressed in their Sunday best, with dresses and khaki pants in abundance. I didn't even *own* anything that would meet their level of appropriate. I had never felt so much like a fish out of water. I sat in the circle, my face a bright tomato red. I can't tell you a thing that was discussed. I didn't know any of the Bible stories, and I was counting the minutes until the service ended. I wanted to be a part of their world, but the shame of *my* world was too great. I decided church wasn't for me and vowed never to return. I knew my place in the world—and it wasn't in that little church.

A week later, I was sleeping over at one of the neighbor's when I felt a hand gently shake me awake. My friend's mother was standing by the side of the bed and leaned down to whisper, "Gina, wake up, sweetie. Your mom has been in a bad accident. You need to go back to your grandparents' house." My mind jolted from fuzzy to alert. She was the "neighborhood mom," who didn't work and haphazardly took care of the roaming children who wandered the street. She was short and plump, with a pixie haircut and spectacles half an inch thick. She was one of those "hands off" mothers who let her kids run in and out of the house and do as they pleased. She would yell with a shrill voice for someone to either stop annoying her or go fetch something. To see concern on her face this night worried me even more.

My grandparents were both teary-eyed as I arrived at their home across the street. My mom had been on her way home from working the late shift and was hit by a semi-trailer truck from the side when she was turning off the highway into the neighborhood.

We changed clothes and headed to the hospital, where my mom was in ICU. As we were heading down the hallway, we walked past the hospital chapel. I peaked in and saw a few rows of seats and a spotlighted big white cross. A few people were sitting quietly with their heads bowed. By this time, God was no longer "anonymous" to me, but I still didn't understand the power He has to heal and transform. I knew Christians said Jesus was the Son of God, but I didn't think that belief was real. Still, I was drawn to that cross. I wanted to go in and pray, but I was too afraid of being judged. This little voice in my head said those weren't *my* people in the chapel. God was reserved for people who knew how to pray and had the Bible stories committed to memory.

I walked in to the room where my mother lay unconscious, fearing what I might see. Would there be blood? Scars? Bruises? Would I recognize her or be able to communicate with her? As I walked closer, I silently prayed, *Please, God, if you save her, I will believe in You.* With my young brain I thought I could negotiate with the Almighty Father in Heaven. *I will eat my peas, if you let me have candy after dinner.* All children may think like this. I have given birth and raised two experts in the skills of negotiation. Payback.

My mother spent days recovering in the hospital but eventually made it home with relatively minor neck and back injuries. The real, unspoken injury was the grief of losing her baby boy and having to bury him. That injury stayed with her much longer.

As I look back at my childhood and teen years, there were moments sprinkled in where I felt God calling for me, but I continued to negotiate with Him: *If You do this, God, then I'll believe.* When I was thirteen, the Lord placed a friend in my life who was a Christian. She was a free spirit with long, dark hair, olive skin, and the sweetest temperament I had ever known. She was "all in" for Jesus. She often spoke to me about Him. She invited me to church and her youth group activities. Even through my cynicism, I was attracted to the goodness I saw in her. I attended church with her a few times, and during one of the Sunday services, the congregation shared communion. I had never seen anything like it. They were all breaking off a piece of bread from one loaf and drinking grape juice from little plastics cups. I asked my friend if I should take communion, and to my surprise, she said no.

"You know I don't think you should unless you are saved," she said.

What did that even mean? I believed there was a God. I kept praying to Him. Wasn't that enough? One evening, I had an opportunity to speak privately with the youth group leader. I told the story of my mother's accident and praying for God to heal her. He just nodded and mumbled something un-inspirational. He never offered to pray with me. I often wonder, *Were those opportunities not in God's timing? Had the ones serving Him failed to fulfill their mission?*

The back-and-forth tug-of-war between me and God continued for twelve years. Finally God said, "Enough is enough," and placed the perfect person in my life to lead me to the truth: my husband, Ken.

In late 2004, I moved to Dallas, Texas. I was the first in my immediate family to go to college and graduate with a four-year degree, but I continued to waffle on what to do with my life. A series of poor choices left me living in a small town in Louisiana, about three hours east of Dallas. Now at a crossroads, I could either stay or start over somewhere else. Going back to Florida was out of the question. I had escaped my past and wanted to make it in a city where I didn't know a soul.

I attended a film festival at the Dallas Museum of Art, contemplating getting back into the acting world I had been a part of in college. Most actors I knew up to that point were lost, insecure souls, seeking approval from wherever they could get it. They weren't judgmental or presumptive, and most importantly, they were *weird*. For someone who lived inside of her head and felt shy and out-of-place like I did, the acting community provided a warm blanket of acceptance.

I was standing beside the bar at the opening night reception, not knowing anyone, and up walks my future husband. We talked all night and then met for breakfast the next day, which turned into lunch, which turned into dinner. He was unlike anyone I had dated before. Ken was a single father of two, ages six and seven. He had gone through two marriages and two divorces. He said he was a Christian, but I assumed he meant he was a good person and sometimes attended church. That was the type of Christian I mostly encountered, the CEOs of the faith (Christmas and Easter Only). However, he was serious. He invited me to go to church with him and the kids one Sunday. And then the next Sunday. And then every Sunday.

Okay, this is what we do now? was my initial reaction. But I quickly grew to love it. This church experience was different from those in the past. I was hearing for the first time that God loves everyone. He *loves* the broken, the hurting, the cynical, the emotionally needy, the emotionally distant, the self-sufficient. He loves us all—and equally. Despite the hurt and pain we have been through, despite the hurt and pain we have *caused*, He still loves us. I finally understood why I had always felt drawn toward God. He was calling for me even before I knew who He was.

One evening, Ken and I were discussing the Christian faith. I could tell he wanted to say more. Finally, he asked if I wanted to know what it meant to be saved, what the whole thing was about, and how to pray for it. I said yes, and he laid out the entire Bible, from Genesis to Revelation. Then he asked if I wanted to pray. I was unsure for a moment, because of those generic thoughts about Christianity being a bunch of rules that restrict your life and your happiness. The cynic in me often rears her ugly head and stops pure joy in her tracks. I pushed through the cynicism and knelt to pray. I accepted Christ into my life, and He changed me in an instant.

Since that moment fourteen years ago, my world has transformed. The need for others' love and approval has slowly dissipated, and God has given me the family that I desired as a child. I now have contentment and joy in a way that I never knew before. This is not to say life is perfect. While we live in this world, there will be trials and tribulations. That's a guarantee. However, peace now exists where there was once anxiety. Unconditional love overflows. And there is hope that there will one day be no more pain—only joy—as I sit at the feet of my Father in Heaven.

God is with us and calling us. Can you hear Him?

Gina Morrison *lives in Dallas, Texas with her husband of thirteen years, two kids, two step-kids, and a dog. She likes writing things that make people laugh, bring people together, inform them, or make them think about life and faith in a new light—without trying to be controversial. There's enough of that in the world.*

Thoughts to Ponder
from God Is Calling

1. God calls all of us throughout our lives.

2. When someone we know is seeking God, we should offer to pray with them to receive Jesus.

3. God continues to pursue us until we say yes.

**Over the years,
how has God called you?**

---

*My sheep listen to my voice; I know them,
and they follow me. — John 10:27*

Do You Ever Feel Alone?

by Jane Keller

I was afraid a monster was under my bed. When I was six years old, I ran and jumped into my bed and pulled the covers up over my head. I didn't dare let my fingers or toes dangle over the edge of the bed, because the monster might bite or grab them. I folded the sheets around my face to make a hole to breathe through, and then I tried not to move and go to sleep. Can you imagine the horror? I was all alone with a monster under my bed.

Fifty years later, I was lying in bed, hugging my Bible and praying to God to heal me of a cancer that had taken over my body. I wanted to cover myself in the sheets and hide from the scary monster. However, just like when I was a child, there was no hiding.

I had been diagnosed with Diffuse Large B-cell Lymphoma. The tumor was the size of a softball in my abdomen, and the cancer had spread to lymph nodes in other parts of my body. One of my lungs was filled with fluid. After the biopsies, tests, and lung drainings, I settled in for five months of thirteen medications through my veins to kill the cancer cells. I had all the side-effects, from hair loss to dehydration, tingling hands and feet, and fatigue. Every time I received a round of chemo, I became neutropenic, which meant I had no immune system, and going out in public wasn't safe.

We had just poured the foundation for our new house, and I wondered if I would ever live there. Not only was I unable to be a part of building our new dream home, but I was also unable to carry my portion of work in the business my husband and I had bought, which was why we moved to Louisiana. To add to the aloneness, I was getting treatment in Minnesota, a two-day drive from home. Because of the neutropenia, it wasn't safe for me to fly.

My husband, family, friends, church, and medical care team were with me every step of the way. But some of them were far away. No one could be there with me, comforting me during the long, dark nights.

I realized I couldn't live my life afraid of imaginary monsters under my bed. I had to face what I was afraid of, which was the same thing I was afraid of when I was six years old—aloneness and death. Death was frightening because it was the ultimate "alone" experience.

As a child, I learned that people died, and it was scary. When I walked by a church on my way to grade school, the front doors were open in preparation for a funeral. I glanced through the doors and down the aisle. A man was lying motionless in a casket. I regretted looking and tried to forget what I had seen. I saw movies depicting Jesus' crucifixion, and thinking about Him dying scared me. Death was too horrible, dark, and lonely. I feared the death that no one could save me from.

Reality hit me again when my father died. I felt like a part of me had died, and I would never get that part back until I died and was reunited with him in Heaven. A hole was left inside of me, where his laughter, unconditional love, and desire for the best for me had lived, but now it was gone. Who would "be in my corner?" Who would always welcome me with open arms, often with applause? Who would ensure that our family was taken care of? There would be no family leader without Dad. Furthermore, I would be alone without my dad.

While I was in bed, hugging my Bible and praying to God to heal me of my cancer, all these times of needing a Savior came to a culmination. Why was I begging God? What was I so afraid of? Death and aloneness again? I realized that I was completely helpless. I decided right then and there to let God take complete control of my life. I gave up trying so hard on my own. It finally struck me that I had never been in control. He always has been. I had to be put in this situation so I could see the truth and trust Him fully.

Everything changed when I prayed, "God, I know You love me. I know You want what's best for me. Thank You for bringing me closer to You through whatever trial You choose— even if it's cancer." I felt like a warm rush of soothing water was flowing through me, filling me from head to toe, leaving perfect peace and joy. It was an act of faith. Cancer was not the enemy. It was not the monster. It was my unwillingness to let go and trust God completely. That was the real monster. It took cancer for me to realize how much deeper my relationship with God could be—how much happier and peaceful I could be.

Now I could see other people through His perspective—all of them in need of love. And I could see myself from His perspective—a person needing His love and comfort. I've heard it said that "one does not discover new lands without consenting to lose sight of the shore for a very long time." This is how I felt. I was beginning a new journey into whatever lay ahead. It could be suffering and pain and death. Nevertheless, I was ready to stop worrying and start trusting. I was already a Christian, but God became much more real, and my relationship with Him deepened that night.

I had accepted Christ when I was a child. If I asked Jesus to come into my life, I was "saved" and would go to Heaven. I learned this in Sunday school. When I was six years old, my father preached a sermon on Easter Sunday that talked about God loving everyone unconditionally. Just think, at all times, God is actively loving us. The Bible says in Psalm 146, "He upholds the cause of the oppressed and gives food to the hungry. The Lord sets prisoners free, the Lord gives sight to the blind, the Lord lifts up those who are bowed down, the Lord loves the righteous. The Lord watches over the foreigner and sustains the fatherless and the widow."

This message can penetrate any heart, and it did mine. My father went on to explain that God loved us and sent His Son so we can find forgiveness and new life through Him. However, we have all sinned and are separated from God and need forgiveness. But God provided a way for us by sending His Son Jesus to die for our sin. Jesus rose from the dead and is alive today. God clearly tells us that Jesus is the only way to salvation. All we need to do is accept His gift of eternal life by faith. When we give ourselves to Christ, God gives us His Spirit and makes all things new. I wanted to walk down the aisle to the front the church when my father asked people to accept Christ, but I was afraid.

Later that night, when we were back at home and I was in bed, I couldn't take the fear of being alone and dying any longer. I was tired of fearing the "monsters," and I wanted to know God's love better. I got out of bed, went down the stairs, and knocked on my parents' bedroom door. I told my dad that I wanted to ask Jesus into my life so that when I died, I would go to Heaven. He knelt alongside me at my bed and led me in a simple prayer.

I repeated the words after him. "Dear Jesus, I know I am a sinner. I know You died for me on a cross, so my sins could be forgiven. I ask You to forgive me of my sins and come into my life. I give myself to You. In Jesus' name, amen." I immediately felt a warm rush from my head to my feet. I was relieved and happy. If I died then, I would go to Heaven with the rest of my family, friends, and people in church. It was as simple as that. From that day on, I have never doubted my relationship with God, questioned the security of eternal life in Heaven, or wondered if God loved me.

Brokenness shapes character and prepares us to serve effectively. I think God allows His children to experience pain for a reason. He molds us and grows us spiritually through pain. He teaches us about Himself and reveals more about ourselves in the process. The trials that I don't understand are times when I can ask God to teach me His lessons. He has responded with gentleness and love. With the Holy Spirit as my comforter, I have more joy and peace than I could have imagined.

A book in the Bible, James, says to consider trials joy, because they produce patience. However, my favorite verse since childhood comes from 1 Peter 1:7—"These [trials] have come so that the proven genuineness of your faith—of greater worth than gold, which perishes even though refined by fire— may result in praise, glory and honor when Jesus Christ is revealed."

When I chose that verse as my favorite, I told my mother. She knew the verse well, and asked, "Are you sure that's your favorite verse, Jane? That's not an easy verse to live up to." I wanted to sear it onto my heart as my favorite Bible verse. My mom didn't know it, but she showed me what strong faith was when I was a child.

My mother walked through the "test of fire" many times. I have learned more about faith from her example than anyone else I can think of, yet through it all, her joy increased. In the valley of brokenness, God tenderly picks up our shattered pieces and remolds them in the image of His Son, Jesus.

Did you ever notice that God's Kingdom is upside down, compared to the world? Once we've been transformed by God, we desire to respect, serve, and sacrifice for others. We have been changed to want to listen, fill others' needs, and forgive. We encourage complete strangers. We want to bless our enemies, do good for people who hurt us, and live peaceably. It is not our normal instinct to show joy, gratefulness, and thanksgiving. Humility, mercy, and compassion are God-given traits. When our lives are directed by God, that is the way we want to behave. We choose to do what He wants, and the more we do that, the more natural it becomes.

When I finished cancer treatments, my husband and I drove from Minnesota back to our home in Louisiana. One of my favorite things to look at in the city where we live is three large white crosses in a field by a church along the Interstate. When I see the crosses, I smile, and my soul wants to sing because they are my "Statue of Liberty." At the cross, my heart was set free.

The empty cross is the symbol of love and redemption, a place where anyone can go and be rescued, find forgiveness, and receive eternal life. The cross is the symbol that we are never alone. The crosses stand over the church. We drove past the crosses to the new house that my husband worked so hard to build. It wasn't quite finished yet, but it was like walking into a dream come true.

Did you know that God has prepared a city for us? You can go there when you die. You can have eternal security. You can go to bed tonight and not worry about death. The God of the universe invites you to know Him. Will you make that decision today? Why wait? All you must do is believe Him. Admit that you are a sinner and that you need Him. Ephesians 2:8–9 says, "For it is by grace you have been saved, through faith—and this is not from yourselves, it is the gift of God— not by works, so that no one can boast." Are you willing to give your life to Him and begin a new life of freedom from aloneness? The One Who created you knows how to love you best. This is a personal decision. No one else can make it for you.

When we give ourselves to Christ, God gives us His Spirit and makes all things new. Nothing can separate us from God's love. He specialized in the impossible.

By the way, my cancer is in complete remission. I can forget the past and look forward to a future without fear, trusting in God's plan for me. No matter what happens, I know I'm never alone.

Jane Keller is just another person, a pilgrim, trying to make her way through this life until she sees Jesus. God has placed her and her husband in their business in Baton Rouge, Louisiana. She has lived in many states and had the privilege of being a missionary kid in Mexico. Jane has had many jobs, particularly in the restaurant industry, where she learned many lessons growing up. She is going wherever God leads. To God be the glory.

Thoughts to Ponder
from Do You Ever Feel Alone?

1. With God on your side, there is no reason to fear the monsters of life.

2. When you give your heart to Jesus, you are never alone.

3. Trials mold us to be more like God.

What "monsters" lurk in your life?

There is no fear in love.
But perfect love drives out fear. — 1 John 4:18

The Masks Women Wear

by Tammy Pearce Nix

As I imagine who's reading my story, I see each of your beautiful faces. I see your care in your makeup, your hair styled just right, and your smile. I even notice that your outfit is nicely "put together." However, I can't help but wonder—what masks are you wearing today? What life events might we share?

We put on the *perfect* mask each time we gather with friends and acquaintances. You know what I'm talking about. When asked, "How are you?" the standard answer is, "Great! Life is great," or "This weather . . ." We say anything—except what we've just struggled with before we walked in the door or about what kept us up at night. Even with our *dearest* friends, we maintain the mask of "life is great."

One day, my mask crumbled and fell to the floor. It was the day I admitted for the first time that I was not "okay." In February 2004, I began attending a large church where I could sit unobtrusively "in the middle of the middle." I was visible only to a few neighboring folks, who greeted me as I sat down. I was not in the back where I would have to smile at everybody passing by, and I was certainly not in the front row. Just in the middle. That way, I was lost in the sea of faces, lest someone ask too many friendly questions.

However, where I was sitting didn't matter when I heard an important announcement that would change my life forever. The church was starting small group meetings on Sunday evenings. I looked around. Did anyone else feel the pull of that announcement? The goal was to gather with a few people and discuss an assigned topic. They were starting with a book study of *The Purpose Driven Life* by Rick Warren. What would it hurt? I signed up to attend at a couple's home close to where I lived with my mom and stepdad.

At the first meeting, nine strangers were seated around the table. The host asked, "So, tell us about you." When it was my turn, that's all it took. Suddenly, my mouth opened, and I said, "My name is Tammy, and I've been through hell." Did I mention that it was *the* first time I had been able to be honest about my life?

You see, just like some of you, I had been through some hard things. Before, I had been able to "gloss over" and maintain my "life is great" mask, especially in a room full of strangers. No one—not my family, colleagues, nor church friends—no one knew the girl behind the mask. I had not shared the hard, deep, life events with anyone. I was thirty-five and had never made a friend that I trusted enough to share my guilt and shame. I carried it alone. I carried it until I couldn't carry it anymore.

A year earlier, my son passed away in his sleep. His fifteenth birthday would have come at the end of the month. I couldn't look our group leader in the eye and tell him, "Life is great." That host couple and another couple became my first friends. Trisha and Angelika, especially, were the first friends I trusted. I've since learned the value of friends like them. They loved me without the dreaded judgment. They laughed with me and cried with me. Most importantly, they walked with me on the journey to healing and transparency.

Today, instead of hiding behind a mask, I can share about how angry I was at God for taking my son. The doctors gave no reasonable medical explanation. The death certificate said, "Died of natural, unknown causes." How does that happen to someone so young? He went to sleep one night at our house, then woke up the next day in Heaven. How I resented God for taking someone so precious to me.

The months after RJ's death were the first time in my life that I was honest in conversations with my Creator. I didn't utter "socially acceptable" prayers. Oh no. I cried ugly and wailed at the emotions that raged inside me. Until one day. A life-changing encounter with my Savior.

I remember being in a heartfelt outburst and picturing a story in the Bible—the one where hurricane winds threatened to overtake the boat and drown every man in it. With just three words, Jesus stood and calmed the waves. "Peace. Be still." Just like the story, my raging emotions calmed. That's been six years ago now, and I've never felt that way again.

Somehow, my anger and angst of losing my son was rolled together with events in my childhood that were beyond my control and then replaced with a calmness of spirit. Yes, there are still difficult times that bring raw emotions, but not like that. The feeling of uncontrolled rage and grief? It's gone. I cannot imagine going through that experience without having the peace and comfort of Jesus to walk with me to still those raging emotions. I don't know if I could have survived that experience without Him.

Peeling back the layers of my once "secure as Fort Knox" mask has been a journey, because I had spent a lifetime applying those layers. My family moved around so much when I was a child that I attended eight different schools. Sometimes, I attended two schools within one year. Each move brought new adventures, new neighborhoods to explore, and new opportunities to put on a different mask. I didn't think about it then. I just did it.

Maybe it was a practice learned by hanging out at the beauty shops where my mom worked. I heard all the ladies talk about whether another woman's hair, makeup, or outfit was "perfectly coordinated." It might have been from overhearing the same conversations at the church ladies' events. I don't know. I wasn't paying much attention to any of that, because I was a tomboy who learned to ride horses, hunt, and fish. I played pool at the bars where I hung out with my dad, while my mom worked on Saturdays. I was just like my father in those days. Definitely a daddy's girl, I had no idea that the reason for all the "new adventures" in my young life were *not* due to the "Gypsy blood in our veins." I know now that the root was really my dad's alcohol addiction. He couldn't deal with things in his life, so he did what he saw his father do. He drank to cover them up—until he couldn't. Then he would quit that job and get a fresh start in a new town, either in Texas, where my mom was from, or in Arkansas, where he grew up.

In recent years, I've shared about the sexual abuse inflicted on me by members of my extended family, beginning at age five. Even harder to face were the decisions and actions driven by the guilt and shame of the "game" started by my uncle. You know, the feeling where if people ever found out, they would know how "bad" I was. The feelings of being "dirty" and "ashamed" grew as I got older and understood more about what had happened.

I was driven to be involved in as many school activities as possible. I was a cheerleader for eight years. I was on the drill team, debate team, and drama team. I was a member of the science club, French club, and Honor Society. I took all the advanced classes. Without putting forth much effort, I was an excellent student. I was surrounded by people, but I felt alone. This was the way it was for most of my life.

As an adult, I thrived in sales and support positions. I networked and traveled. I trained teams and spoke easily and confidently to groups of different sizes. All I had to do was put on whatever mask was needed.

Let's return to the school days. I'm amazed and grateful for the protection I received from the drug and alcohol scene. Thankfully, I was too busy for that. Or if I attended the bonfire parties, I was the one driving my friends home, because I really didn't enjoy the taste of cheap beer or strawberry wine.

Before my senior year, something changed. From the time I was fourteen, I had been working at different little places. That summer, with grownup makeup, hair, and outfit, I lied about my age and got a job at President's Health Club, working with "grownups in their twenties." These grownups went to bars, drank, and had sex with strangers. I was tired of being the "good one" who didn't do that stuff. I was ready for the "big time." What was I thinking?

One night, I accompanied a group to a bar, picked out a guy, and went home with him. That was the day I found out I wasn't a virgin. At seventeen, with no knowledge of my virginity, my world came crashing down. I had "stuffed" the abuse by my uncles so deep in my subconscious that I couldn't recall that very important detail. I still don't remember all that happened between ages five and twelve.

That began the downward spiral of promiscuity, as well as involvement and marriage to a guy who seemed "safe." At age twenty-two, I found myself divorced with two young children to support, unable to depend on child support. I was working two jobs, including working nights at bars. I was outgoing, vivacious, and made a lot of money. At second-grade cheerleader tryouts, my mom said, "Look them in the eye and smile." That advice was paying off. However, I was still miserable. I was looking for love in more wrong places than I could count, which resulted in two unplanned pregnancies.

I wish I could say I have a family of four beautiful children, but that's not the case. Fear and desperation led to ending the first pregnancy at six weeks. I carried a lot of guilt and shame after that. The second baby was adopted by a wonderful, godly family and raised with love and privileges I could never have provided. My lifestyle was *not* working well for me. I had to get out of the bar scene and raise my two children right.

And I did.

After dropping my goal of finishing nursing school, I obtained a quick certificate to be a medical assistant. That led to several positions in and around the medical field. During that time, I felt God nudging me into a real relationship with Him. I am grateful that I had been baptized at age seven and knew a little about what life was *supposed* to look like.

I knew that life was supposed to be better than what I had experienced. I began searching for the existence I dreamed about. Little did I know that while my mom was driving my kids to Sunday school each week, they were praying for me. Don't ever discredit the prayers of children or the power of a praying momma.

I joined a small church and began working in every area that I could. I figured that if they and God saw all my good works, all the sin and shame of my past would somehow cancel out. Every time the door was open, I was at church, even traveling to conferences with the pastors. At home, I was a scared, angry, single mom, eaten up with responsibility of raising kids by myself, still bearing the shame of my mistakes and failures. My kids bore the brunt of my anger, because they were the closest to me. We struggled daily. My daughter learned to put on that mask and hold it tight. No one knew the violent abuse she had suffered until six months after the abuser committed suicide. I had no idea that my curse had affected my brown-eyed, curly-haired girl.

Today, I am grateful that I never seriously thought about ending my life, although some days would have been easier not to live—to curl into a ball and simply stop breathing. But that didn't happen. If that had occurred when it seemed the easiest, then I wouldn't be married to the amazing husband I now have. I wouldn't know or have the chance to speak life over my two beautiful granddaughters. And I certainly wouldn't have been around to witness the amazing accomplishments of my daughter, despite all odds being stacked against her.

If there's one thing to remember from my story, it's this: only the faithfulness and grace of Jesus have gotten me through the hard seasons in my life. Only He could provide a personal identity of who I really am and end my gut-wrenching quest for "more in life." He told me I am His. I am so valuable to Him that He paid the ultimate price so I could join Him in Heaven for eternity.

Only He can give me the courage to share with you the story of a life once so filled with shame that I couldn't imagine ever taking off the mask in front of you. He alone gives me hope and peace, assuring me that I will see my son again in eternity.

What masks do you wear? Is it time to take them off and let the love of Jesus penetrate your soul? He has the power to heal us from the most difficult tragedies in life, and He gives us the power to truthfully say, "I'm not okay. What about you?"

Tammy Pearce Nix is a native Texan. She loves returning home to the Dallas area, no matter how far she may roam. She and her husband, James, share their home with Katie and Shiloh, their fur babies. Tammy enjoys spending time with and supporting her daughter and granddaughters in their various adventures. A heart for Jesus and her love of horses will soon combine to bring hope, healing, and restoration in a ranch setting.

Thoughts to Ponder
from The Masks Women Wear

1. Nothing is hidden in God's sight.

2. It is healing to be transparent and remove our masks.

3. God provides friends to help us overcome our pain.

What masks do you wear?

Therefore each of you must put off falsehood and speak truthfully to your neighbor, for we are all members of one body. — Ephesians 4:25

Hope Floats
by Tracy Winkles

I love old-fashioned root beer floats, the ones with the frosty mug filled with rich buttery vanilla ice cream topped with sweet root beer soda, creating the ultimate foam that melts in your mouth. Can you taste it? Remember the last time you had one?

Life is a lot like those delicious root beer floats. It is so important to have the right ingredients in order to create the flavor, foam, and taste. However, in my own life I am not sure I had the right ingredients. I was raised in a loving home by my grandparents, a mom and dad, aunts, and uncles. They were all a part of what I considered the perfect life. At the age of fifteen, while attending a winter skiing church camp in New Mexico, I became a "Christian." It fulfilled my dying grandmother's wish for all her grandchildren to be saved so she would see us in Heaven. When she passed from a long battle with cancer on November 1, 1985, my world changed. I had no hope of feeling that love again. I ran from Christianity and church, turning to a lifestyle of drinking and partying with friends.

Ten years later, I married my love, Allan, and we had two boys. I struggled with severe post-partum depression and found that depression ran deep in the women of my family. In 2002, Allan was diagnosed with Type 2 diabetes and almost died after being bit by a rattlesnake at our country ranch. As I sat across the table from the physician who treated him, I was told, "If Allan doesn't take care of himself, you will be a single mom by the time you are fifty." That was a sobering experience. It was then I returned to my faith and started pursuing a relationship and lifestyle for my boys, where church and God were at the center. We were regular attendees, and I was a great volunteer.

As the years passed, we struggled in our marriage. We were caught up in the routines, work, kids, and our romance sank to the bottom of the glass. Somewhere between paying bills, PTA, and doing laundry, I felt alone and lost. I sought help through anti-depression, anxiety, and sleeping pills—anything I could find to make my life seem more perfect. I found my groove.

I had a great job, a hubby who loved me, and two wonderful

boys who were becoming young men. Everything was going too well. I was an active member in a church and volunteered a lot. However, in 2010, I lost my job due to downsizing in corporate America. After fifteen years of dedicated work, my plan of retiring from the company was gone. Once again, I felt hopeless.

During this time of unemployment, I rededicated my life to Jesus and devoted time to His Word. I became more than a member of a church. I now had a relationship with God. I dusted off my Bible and opened it to the verse, Jeremiah 29:11, "'For I know the plans I have for you' declares the Lord, 'plans to prosper you and not to harm you, plans to give you hope and a future.'" *Really, He has plans for me? How could that be?* Life became more meaningful, and both my boys came to know Jesus as their Savior.

Surprisingly, my world fell apart after this stretch of rededication. My husband had a heart attack on February 26, 2017. I was scared and dropped to my knees. When standing in a women's bathroom, I heard my son, Clayton, on the other side of the wall, crying out to God, "Please save my dad, Jesus. He needs You." One week later, my husband suffered another heart attack in my car. I prayed a childlike prayer for God to save him. I could not do this alone.

We had a senior in high school and Connor, our sophomore, adored his Dad. The Lord came through once again, and Allan was home with the boys for an entire week. He had never spent that kind of time with the boys.

I went to a counseling session because the tears had come back in abundance, and I could not understand why. I asked my counselor, "How much more does God think I can handle? If He knows the plan and promises to prosper me, then what is He preparing me for? Something great has to be in the works, right?" After that session, I will never again ask God how much He thinks I can handle again. Never.

Saturday, March 25, was a standard busy spring day. Allan went to work. I sent the boys off to a high school fishing tournament and attended training for my summer part-time job with the Texas Rangers. I wanted to go to the awards ceremony of the fishing tournament, but my schedule wouldn't allow it, which made me furious. I got a text from Clayton: *Mom, today was awesome. I placed and am getting an award.* I felt horrible not attending, but he told me, "Don't worry, Mom. God's got this." I waited at home for everyone to return. Later, Clayton left for a concert in Fort Worth with friends, but not before giving me a huge kiss on the forehead and reminding me, "Smile! God's got this."

Our evening was quiet, and I went to bed early, only to be awakened by Allan asking, "Where is Clayton?" Clayton was past curfew, and Allan was worried. I grabbed my phone to see he had texted multiple times. He was granted backstage passes to meet the artist. He was safe and so happy. I got up to wait on him just after 1 a.m. We texted several times, and at 2:36 he called. "Mom, I had the best day of my life. I placed at the fishing tournament. I got to dance with Maycie, his girl, and meet Aaron Watson. Even better, he is a Christian who shared his faith. Mom, he quoted scriptures."

Clayton was on cloud nine. I told him to be safe, and I would see him when he got home. I dozed off while waiting, and when I woke up at 3:20 a.m., I began texting and calling. No response. It seemed very unreal. I had a huge gaping feeling that something was wrong.

I awakened Allan. I was afraid he would have another heart attack after just now being able to return to work. We woke up Connor so he and I could go look for his brother. Not two blocks from the house, police cars were blocking the road. I saw Clayton's truck. I got out of my car and said to the officer, "That is my son's truck. Where is Clayton?"

The officer knew my name.

I fell to my knees on the double yellow line in the middle of the road and cried bitterly. But I knew one thing. My last text to Clayton at 3:46 a.m. said, *Son, I don't know where you are, but I know wherever it is, God's got you. I just need to hear your voice, so please call me back.*

You see, I knew God had my boy. The next few hours were a blur. I remember these things:

- God had my boy.
- God's plans have a purpose.
- People need Jesus to be able to weather stuff.

Everything. The big stuff, the small stuff, and all the stuff.

I went home that day and threw away all my anti-depression, anxiety, and sleeping pills. I did not want to need anything but Jesus. No one else could get me through this massive pain and horrible heartache. Only Jesus would show me how to help hundreds of friends deal with the loss, strengthen Clayton's brother, and be sure Allan did not die from a broken heart.

I have now been chemically free for nineteen months. My love for Jesus and my faith give me hope. One day, I will see my boy again. Allan is still not 100 percent. He battles with depression and health issues, but we fight to ensure our marriage makes it through the toughest of losses. I have been blessed with friends, family, a job, and a financial future, because God has allowed the relationships and opportunities to come my way.

- I pray daily.
- I cry daily.
- I smile daily.

I don't have it all together, but Jesus and I have a purpose and a plan to make it through each day. Remember, when you find yourself at a new beginning, just give hope a chance to float up.

And it will.

Tracy Winkles is an active wife, mother, and community member in Arlington, Texas. She was challenged to find "faith" and developed a passion for serving during her time as a young adult. After the loss of her son, she started the #Great11 movement, encouraging others to perform 11 acts of kindness for nothing in return. Tracy serves in the community and speaks publicly about faith and living life to the fullest. To find out more, follow her on Facebook, Twitter, or Instagram. Email: **GreatElevenMovement@gmail.com.**

Thoughts to Ponder
from Hope Floats

1. If we seek hope, it will always float to the top.

2. God hears the cries of His people.

3. Only Jesus can carry us through deep grief.

When have you experienced hope during a great trial?

Those who hope in the Lord will renew their strength. They will soar on wings like eagles; they will run and not grow weary, they will walk and not be faint. — Isaiah 40:31

No Longer an Orphan
by Vivian Rogers

You can't change your past, but what you do today can change your future. Sometimes we enter this world fighting for our lives.

My mother was a depraved drug addict and didn't turn away from her addiction while pregnant, so I weighed three pounds at my premature birth, an addict baby, infused with heroin, cocaine, and meth. I was also HIV positive. Satan was determined to take me out this world, but God had other plans.

In those early moments of suffering, my mother wasn't allowed to hold me, because she was so high on drugs. After she became sober, the hospital released me into her care. Even though she had a new daughter to care for, she craved more drugs. As a result, she did the unthinkable and sold me to men so she could buy drugs. I wasn't yet a year old when the sexual abuse began.

What do people do when their home is no longer their *home?* What if that home was never truly safe? Do they have the strength to get up, walk out, and turn their back on all they know? Would they simply lose hope and quit?

These were questions that ripped at my heart throughout childhood. Everyone has a different definition of what a family is and how it operates. The dictionary defines family as a group of individuals living under one roof, who usually share the same DNA. In my case, I defined my family as "untrustworthy." A daughter is supposed to be able to look up to her mom and dad with respect. She should be protected, nurtured, and treated with care. I experienced none of that, but entered another huge nightmare: I was placed in the foster care system as a one-year-old.

Not every foster home is bad, but the one I was placed in was far from good. I became a new daughter to a white German woman who had fostered 257 kids. Despite being so young, I realized that our skin colors weren't the same. The transition for me was culture shock, and her behavior wasn't much different from my biological mother.

My foster mother knew how to play the system well. I was placed in this foster home with twenty-five brothers and sisters. She took in broken kids for the financial benefits, not to love them. She was making $45,000 each month. She was physically and emotionally abusive to most of the kids, except the ones who were disabled and bedridden or were kept alive by machines. She repeatedly told me I was dumb, fat, and ugly. She said I would be a homeless person when I grew up. She locked me in a room for days without food and had my foster siblings make fun of me. When social workers came to the house, I was lucky to eat that day. When the social workers left, I was beaten.

Why is she so cruel? I asked myself.

The trauma created many trust issues. I felt worthless and fearful.

One night while I lay in bed, my foster mother beat me so badly that I could barely breathe. The pain was unbearable. I closed my eyes and . . . Bam! Suddenly, I was in a calm place. I thought it was a dream. It seemed like a dream, but it was real. I felt no more pain, and I was standing in front of a gate. "Welcome," someone said. I didn't look up, because I was afraid. The ground was bright gold. I stayed in one spot and saw hands with holes in the palms reach toward me. "I will never leave you or forsake you. I love you so much," the man said. Giant angels said, "You have to go now." After that experience ended, I felt excruciating pain again.

There are 86,400 seconds and 14,400 minutes in one twenty-four-hour day. I believe we should live every day as if it were our last, because we never know when it will be. When I was nine years old, my foster mother died in a tragic car accident. I thought, *She's gone now. Where am I going to live?*

I had no idea whether things would get better or worse. I didn't want to leave my foster brothers and sisters, who had been part of my life for eight years. I feared for my life, because no one could tell me where we were going. Child Protective Services told us to stay where we were. Our somewhat-mom's husband would take care of us.

Conditions became worse, not better. The man forced me to call him "Dad." When I didn't, I received beatings.

When he moved to East Texas, he only took twelve of us out

of the twenty-five. Everyone thought he was so amazing for taking us in after the tragic loss of our foster mom. But life with him wasn't amazing at all. He hated black kids. He beat us and treated us like trash. He tried to send us to another home, but that never happened. As he sexually abused me, he yelled, "Suck it up, and be a woman."

My young heart hardened. I became depressed and suicidal. My temporary escapes were school and church. My teachers and pastors didn't believe me when I told them I was abused, even though there were numerous signs. My pleas went unheeded.

School and church were better than being at home. My hard heart grew colder. The abuse continued for nineteen years.

My social workers, counselors, and doctors acted like they had no idea what was happening. When I tried to tell them about the abuse, they must have thought I was making everything up. They judged me by my outward appearance and poor behavior.

Did they know what was taking place, but were too afraid to get involved?

Apparently, they believed my foster dad more than me. There was never an investigation of the home. I suffered in silence. I felt like I didn't have a voice that would ever be heard.

Much to everyone's surprise, I graduated from high school and started college when I was nineteen. Unless foster children enroll in college, they are left to their own resources when they turn eighteen. I wanted to excel, but I felt awkward and alienated. I was broken and numb, and I didn't know what to do. I couldn't look at people, because I was carrying the crippling weight of shame, guilt, and trauma. I couldn't respond to my professors' questions. I told God that I was done with Him, and I was going to live my own way.

I knew how to survive, and that's what I did. Honestly, I don't know how I made it that far in life. I definitely didn't want to be a fatal statistic of the foster care system.

The resolve in my mind hardened like concrete. *I must prove everyone wrong who said I couldn't make it to college, I would live in mental hospitals for the rest of my life, or I would be pregnant by age twenty-one.*

There is power in spoken and written words. God states in Proverbs 18:21, "The tongue has the power of life and death, and those who love it will eat its fruit." I breathed deeply and said to myself, *I can do it.* Not one foster youth who has been badly wounded deserves to be thrown away like garbage. Each person is as human and important as the next, but each may have to experience life in a different way.

My first years in college were a struggle because I was carrying a lot of baggage that weighed me down. However, I pushed forward. When I thought I couldn't do it, I sensed something inside me telling me to push on. *He cares for me. He is the only reason that I recently completed my associate degree and am continuing for my bachelor's in social work.*

Despite my abusive beginnings, I realized that God had been the only One who stuck with me. It started to make sense when I heard the voice again say, *I will never leave you or forsake you. I love you so much.* That voice was God's. He had a plan for my life, but so did the enemy.

God also has a plan for your life. He will restore what was taken from you. Joel 2:25 says, "I will repay you for the years the locusts have eaten—the great locust and the young locust, the other locusts and the locust swarm—my great army that I sent among you." Be ready for both the plan of the enemy and God's plan. Pray and be wise enough to know when to resist and flee, and when to stand firm and embrace. The choice is yours, and no one can force you into what you don't want for your life.

I'm living proof that anyone can overcome difficult situations with God on their side. "I can do all this through him who gives me strength" (Philippians 4:13). Believe that you matter to someone. It's your choice whether to stay a victim or live in victory. Don't beat yourself up. You're not alone in your mess. Tell your situation to someone you trust, because someone *will* listen to you. It's okay to speak up and not allow someone else to steal your voice. I learned that not speaking up leaves a lot of room for others to assume incorrect things about you and your circumstances. Silence adds to the pain of bottled-up feelings.

Forgiveness is the key to experiencing freedom. I've learned that when you haven't forgiven those who have hurt you, you take the pains of the past and add them to your future. When you do forgive, you can move forward without that pain.

Give God your ashes, and He will give you beauty. Ashes represent our sorrow, hurt feelings, and disappointments. Let go of the ashes, so you can receive God's beauty. If I hadn't let go of my past, I would never have received the great future I know today. We are meant to overcome the things that have kept us locked up, but it's up to us to allow someone into our life who is trustworthy and desires to help us.

Through your ups and downs, see the light at the end of the tunnel. It took awhile to figure this out, but when I did, I had no limitations. By God's grace, my possibilities are endless. Even when it seems undoable, impossible, or unbearable, I keep walking my healing journey into wholeness. Don't let your past define who you are, and know that, "In this world you will have trouble. But take heart! I have overcome the world" (John 16:33). You can overcome any mountain if you believe God can move it.

I am happy to let you know that I am now twenty-four years old and an overcomer by the blood of Jesus. I am victorious after dealing with HIV/Aids. I have beaten the odds of the foster care system. I have overcome horrific physical and sexual abuse, drugs, and suicidal thoughts. The sexual immorality, preterm birth, and selective mutism are in the past, no longer a part of who I am. If God can do it for me, He can do it for you. Don't give up. He is waiting for you to make the next move.

Only Jesus can turn a mess into a message, a test into a testimony, and a trial into triumph. You can be a victor, not a victim. If God will leave the ninety-nine sheep to save the one who has wandered away, He will search and find you (Matthew 18:12). Stop running or hiding from God, because He will keep pursuing you. He will reveal Himself to you in ways you never imagined. Look up from rock-bottom and meet Him. He will do the rest.

These questions remain: The Master knows you, but do you truly know Him? If you know Jesus, are you following Him and letting Him teach you? Or are you expecting Him to follow you and learn from you?

For so long, I knew of a God but didn't really know Him or allow Him to fully father me. I walked around listening to the devil's lies. I believed I would be an orphan forever, someone nobody ever cared about.

On June 11, 2017, I asked the Lord to be my Father, and I became His princess daughter. From that day forward, I was no longer an orphan. I can say that I am adopted and loved by God.

No matter how your life started, there will be a beautiful ending when you allow God to pen your story. Be "confident of this, that he who began a good work in you will carry it on to completion until the day of Christ Jesus" (Philippians 1:6).

Vivian Rogers was born in Houston, Texas. She is a full-time college student working on her bachelor's degree in social work. She plans to shed a light in the darkest places in the foster care system, giving people a new perspective of life and hope through Jesus Christ.

Thoughts to Ponder

from No Longer an Orphan

1. God can be trusted to love and care for us amid difficult circumstances.

2. By God's grace and His complete forgiveness of our sins, we can forgive others.

3. As a child of God our identity is in Christ, not in what others may think about us.

> **When have you viewed people by their outward appearance rather than by God's heart?**

The Lord does not look at the things people look at. People look at the outward appearance, but the Lord looks at the heart." — 1 Samuel 16:7

What Are You Believing about Yourself, Truth or Lie?

by Amy Hosp

Have you ever believed a lie about yourself? How about multiple lies?

Many times, I have lost focus of who, what, and *how* God wanted me to be. It wasn't until I was willing to seek help and open myself to trusted people that I regained my focus. Instead of being stuck, I moved forward with an understanding of the lies that ruled my life and were destroying me.

What we believe about ourselves isn't always the truth. I learned that keeping secrets about my past was harmful to my future.

I once thought I was a very bad person. I believed several events in my life were my fault, even though they were beyond my control. I didn't want to share them with others, because I was afraid of being rejected. I thought God was rejecting me, but I learned that God always wants to be with me. Through my story, I encourage you to look inside and see if everything you believe is God's truth about you, because embracing lies will keep you stuck in the past.

When I was a seminary student, I went through a stretch of remembering painful childhood things that I had blocked. I developed an eating disorder at a young age. It began as overeating but morphed into starvation. I even blocked out of my memory a time when I was in a treatment program. I had a habit of self-harm, which turned into cutting as an adult—a very dark hatred of my life, laced with suicidal depression.

After the terrorist attack of September 11, 2001, I realized I was not living like I had promised God. I felt called to be a missionary when I was nine years old and spent my childhood focused on this career goal. I moved to New York City one day before 9/11, which was a stopping point before I traveled to Nigeria as a missionary.

The New York news coverage of 9/11 was different from other parts of the country. I saw people escaping the heat of fire in the towers by jumping to their deaths. I felt convicted for disobeying God by ignoring opportunities to witness. If I had been obedient, would my obedience have led to saving one of the desperate souls jumping from the towers? Maybe not, but the point is that I felt very conflicted about not doing my part for God.

I decided to fast so I could repent and refocus my life on what God had called me to do—and then do it. The fast started positively, so much so that I decided to extend it. I've always been a "jump in with both feet" person, giving my all, no matter what. This is not always the smartest way to start huge endeavors in life.

As an overweight person with a long-time eating disorder, I would get excited about anything and everything that would help me lose weight, so it was easy for me to take things a bit too far. In the first week of my fast, I lost a large amount of weight. I felt focused on the Lord and more energetic. A little bit of this good thing would be better if I continued for a longer time. I decided to extend the fast for one more week.

This fast quickly turned to a "let's see how much weight I can lose now" focus. If a person goes without eating for a long time, hunger goes away and only returns when starvation sets in. It was at that point that I saw not only the physical issues that starving caused but also how the depression had intensified.

I was depressed before, but I'm not sure I completely recognized the depression, because I had lived with it for so long. I didn't know what it was like to feel normal. During this "fast," I remembered things I had blocked for so many years and now blamed myself for. Learning that I had blocked out so much increased my self-hate.

I fasted for about a month and removed all food from my house, a rule I lived by for the next nine years. This fast caused incorrect long-term thoughts about eating—thoughts I still struggle with at times. I was eating very little, and I knew things were getting out of control. The spiritual part of the fast had stopped long ago, and not eating became the focus of my life.

I was working with a friend from church. As I talked with her about not eating, she became very concerned and encouraged me to speak with our pastor.

Here are some of the things we talked about:

- I know I am in trouble. Being open and honest is the only way to save my life. I want to share my thoughts before they become too private or out of control.

- I have lost forty pounds, which is both good and bad. I have finally accomplished not overeating, something that I had wanted to do for years.
- I believe, if I control my eating, other things will fall into place.
- I am concerned because of my feelings about 9/11 and what I experienced.
- Most of all, I am concerned about the lack of discipline in my life.
- I feel embarrassed to talk about this, because it is a huge mark of spiritual immaturity.
- I am nervous about opening myself up to the prayer minister, because I don't know her—and trust is not easy for me.
- I am struggling with depression and harmful thoughts due to my control issue of eating.
- I have been eating less than 300 calories a day. When I go over that, I tend to force myself to throw up.
- I feel powerful when I am hungry. I am confused and angered by this, but I don't want to tell anyone. Somehow this secret makes me feel powerful.
- I have neglected living on God's Word. It is no longer about fasting and being hungry, but is about some type of punishment. Being hungry is punishment to me, and I feel the need to punish myself to the extreme because of losing my focus on the fast.
- I feel defeated and guilty because the fast has stopped. Not only did I not accomplish what I wanted, but I see the beginning of some very dangerous things. Even though I recognize it, I don't know how to stop it.
- I want to crawl into a cave and not come out. I spend lots of time sleeping and thinking about how much I am not eating and what I will tell people if they notice.
- My friend keeps telling me that I am thinking backward.
- Being sick has nothing to do with not eating. I've had asthma since living in New York City during 9/11. My regular doctor told me that it was not causing problems but

soon would, which somehow made me feel validated.

My pastor's reply to me was incredible. I had never felt so much love and understanding from someone. He had watched me since I came home from New York. He knew I had been sick and was in and out of the hospital several times. He told me to see a medical doctor and start seeing a counselor at the seminary, which was free for me. He told me how much he loved me and how much he wanted me to be happy, healthy, and whole so I could serve God as He had called me to do.

Thank God for my pastor. He saved my life.

Soon after the meeting with my pastor, I saw a counselor at the seminary and continued for four years. He too was instrumental in saving my life. He saw me through the worst of times, encouraged me with the Word of God, and fed my spirit with love and care. He led me through this journey with great wisdom and understanding, and I came to trust him more than I had ever trusted anyone. One of the things I loved best about him was that he took time to read my journals and ask questions about them to be sure he understood what I was trying to say. Most of the time, I wrote poems as riddles or created pictures as a puzzle instead of just saying what was going on. He was excellent at solving the riddles, rhymes, and puzzles, which allowed me to communicate with him in a way that made me feel safe and accepted. I think back to all I put that man through, and I am amazed that he stuck with me for so long.

Psalm 107 reminds us that God has delivered from the fog of feeling that we cannot find or remember what God has done for us. I'm not sure how I came to believe the lies about myself, but that is not important. The important part is that I was willing to challenge those lies.

I would not have been able to do this if it weren't for my pastor, my friend, the prayer minister, and my counselor loving me enough to help me. I had to be willing to open myself up, and yes, it took several years for me to do this. In doing so, my life completely changed, and I can serve God with confidence.

Are you willing to open your heart and see God's Truth about you that destroys the harmful lies you believe about yourself?

Amy Hosp *grew up in Frisco, Texas. She is a graduate of Dallas*

Christian College with a B.S. in Ministry & Leadership. She has worked toward earning a master's degree at Southwestern Baptist Theological Seminary in Fort Worth, Texas. Amy is a writer, photographer, musician, and missionary. She deals with life by always looking for the positive side to every situation. Her passion is to challenge the minds of others to look deep inside of themselves, see life from a better perspective, and find the true giftings of God in their lives. She is the author of Collection of Sketches for Reaching Out to the Hurting and Lost *and* Ehlers Danlos Syndrome with Liberty the Dog.

HospAmy@yahoo.com
TheLibertyOfItAll.com

Thoughts to Ponder

from What Are You Believing about Yourself, Truth or Lie?

1. Always compare what you believe about yourself to what God says about you in His Word.

2. The enemy of our souls will weigh us down with guilt.

3. Godly counsel can help us see more clearly.

What lies are you believing about yourself?

Some wandered . . . were hungry and thirsty, and their lives ebbed away. Then they cried out to the Lord in their trouble, and he delivered them from their distress. — Psalm 107:4-6

Testimony in Scripture
by Anne Worth

I love the Lord, for He heard my voice;
He heard my cry for mercy.
Because He turned his ear to me,
I will call on Him as long as I live.
The cords of death entangled me,
The anguish of the grave came over me;
I was overcome by distress and sorrow.
Then I called on the name of the Lord:
"Lord, save me!"
The Lord is gracious and righteous;
Our God is full of compassion.
The Lord protects the unwary;
When I was brought low, He saved me.
What shall I return to the Lord
For all His goodness to me?
I will fulfill my vows to the Lord
In the presence of all His people.
Psalm 116:1-6, 12, 14

And that is what I have come to do, to fulfill my vow, to tell you God's story in my life through words of Scripture.

The Jews there were amazed and asked,
"How did this man get such learning
"Without having been taught?"
Jesus answered, "My teaching is not my own.
"It comes from the one who sent me."
John 7:15-16

Come and see what God has done,
His awesome deeds for mankind!
Come and hear, all you who fear God;
Let me tell you what He has done for me.
Psalm 66:5, 16

In 1997, I became very ill. I couldn't have gone on without God.

> I am torn between the two:
> I desire to depart and be with Christ,
> Which is better by far;
> But it is more necessary for you
> That I remain in the body.
> *Philippians 1:23*

God had a plan to use me in a way that had not been fulfilled.

> Unless the Lord had given me help,
> I would soon have dwelt in the silence of death.
> When I said, "My foot is slipping,"
> Your unfailing love, Lord, supported me.
> When anxiety was great within me,
> Your consolation brought me joy.
> The Lord has become my fortress,
> And my God the rock in whom I take refuge.
> *Psalm 94:17 19, 22*

> The Lord looked down from His sanctuary on high,
> From heaven He viewed the earth,
> To hear the groans of the prisoners
> And release those condemned to death.
> So the name of the Lord will be declared.
> *Psalm 102:19-21*

In darkness and the deepest gloom, I sat suffering in iron chains of Disbelief and Arrogance, for I had despised the counsel of the Most High. He led me by a straight way to a church where I could settle. He brought me out of darkness and broke away my chains!

> Give thanks to the Lord for His unfailing love
> And His wonderful deeds for mankind,
> For He breaks down gates of bronze
> And cuts through bars of iron.
> Some became fools through their rebellious ways

And suffered affliction because of their iniquities.
Psalm 107:15-17

In my anguish I cried to the Lord, and He answered by sending me to a church retreat, setting me free. I had been praying for death and got it—death to my own ways—death to my self-directed life.

> I was pushed back and about to fall,
> But the Lord helped me.
> The Lord is my strength and my defense;
> He has become my salvation.
> *Psalm 118:13-14*

> I will not die but live, and will proclaim what the Lord has done.
> *Psalm 118:17*

> "Because [Anne] loves Me," says the Lord,
> "I will rescue [her]; I will protect [her],
> "For [she] acknowledges My name.
> "[She] will call on Me, and I will answer [her];
> "I will be with [her] in trouble,
> "I will deliver [her] and honor [her].
> "With long life I will satisfy [her]
> "And show [her] My salvation."
> *Psalm 91:14-16*

On January 28, 1998, Jesus Christ came into a hotel room in Dallas, Texas and called me to follow Him. Prior to that moment, I thought all Christians were judgmental hypocrites. I didn't know I was the judgmental hypocrite.

> Even though I was once a blasphemer
> And a persecutor and a violent [person],
> I was shown mercy because I acted
> In ignorance and unbelief.
> The grace of our Lord was poured out on me abundantly,
> Along with the faith and love that are in Christ Jesus.

Here is a trustworthy saying that deserves full acceptance:
Christ Jesus came into the world to save sinners—
Of whom I am the worst.
But for that very reason I was shown mercy
So that in me, the worst of sinners,
Christ Jesus might display His immense patience
As an example for those who would believe in Him
And receive eternal life.
1 Timothy 1:13-16

At one time we too were foolish, disobedient, deceived
And enslaved by all kinds of passions and pleasures.
But when the kindness and love of God our Savior appeared,
He saved us, not because of righteous things we had done,
But because of His mercy.
Titus 3:3, 4-5

I put off my old self, which was corrupt, and put on the new
self, which was created to be like God, righteous and holy.

He put a new song in my mouth,
A hymn of praise to our God.
Psalm 40:3

For you were once darkness,
But now you are light in the Lord.
Ephesians 5:8

He has filled the hungry with good things
But has sent the rich away empty.
Luke 1:53

With him at my right hand, I will not be shaken.
Therefore my heart is glad and my tongue rejoices;
My body also will rest secure,
Because You will not abandon me to the realm of the dead,
Nor will You let Your faithful one see decay.
Psalm 16:8-10

I know where I came from and where I am going.
John 8:14

He chose us in Him before the creation of the world
To be holy and blameless in His sight.
In love He predestined us for adoption
To sonship through Jesus Christ,
In accordance with His pleasure and will.
Ephesians 1:4-5

God, who is rich in mercy, made us alive with Christ
Even when we were dead in transgressions.
It is by grace you have been saved,
Through faith— and this is not from yourselves,
It is the gift of God—not by works,
So that no one can boast.
For we are God's handiwork,
Created in Christ Jesus to do good works.
Ephesians 2:4-5, 8-10

Although I am less than the least of all the Lord's people,
This grace was given me: to preach . . .
The boundless riches of Christ . . .
According to His eternal purpose
That He accomplished in Christ Jesus our Lord.
Ephesians 3:8-9, 11

Being confident of this,
That He who began a good work in you
Will carry it on to completion
Until the day of Christ Jesus.
Philippians 1:6

Sing, barren woman, you who never bore a child;
Burst into song, shout for joy,
You who were never in labor;
Because more are the children of the desolate woman
Than of her who has a husband.
Do not be afraid; you will not be put to shame.

Do not fear disgrace; you will not be humiliated.
You will forget the shame of your youth.

For your Maker is your husband—
The Lord Almighty is his name—
The Holy One of Israel is your Redeemer.
Isaiah 54:1, 4-5

I was like the woman who had been crippled by a spirit for eighteen years, bent over and unable to straighten up. I could not change myself to become the woman I wanted to be. On the outside, I looked good, but I was so sick on the inside— physically, emotionally, and spiritually.

"Woman, you are set free from your infirmity."
Then [Jesus] put his hands on her,
And immediately she straightened up and praised God.
Luke 13:12-13

For more than twenty years, I had been bound by Satan. But now I was set free. Praise God!

You are my Lord;
Apart from You I have no good thing.
You alone are my portion and my cup;
You make my lot secure.
The boundary lines have fallen for me in pleasant places.
I keep my eyes always on the Lord.
With Him at my right hand, I will not be shaken.
Therefore my heart is glad and my tongue rejoices;
My body also will rest secure.
You will fill me with joy in Your presence.
Psalm 16:2, 5-6, 8-9, 11

I pray that out of His glorious riches
He may strengthen you with power
Through His Spirit in your inner being,
So that Christ may dwell in your hearts through faith.
And I pray that you, being rooted and established in love,

May have power, together with all the Lord's holy people,
To grasp how wide and long and high and deep
Is the love of Christ,
And to know this love that surpasses knowledge—
That you may be filled to the measure of all the fullness of
God.
Ephesians 3:16-19

Pray also for me, that whenever I speak,
Words may be given me so that I will
Fearlessly make known the mystery of the gospel,
For which I am an ambassador.
Ephesians 6:19-20

I proclaim Your saving acts in the great assembly;
I do not seal my lips, Lord.
I speak of Your faithfulness and Your saving help.
Psalm 40:9-10

Sing the praises of the Lord,
You His faithful people; praise His holy name.
His favor lasts a lifetime;
Weeping may stay for the night,
But rejoicing comes in the morning.
You turned my wailing into dancing;
You removed my sackcloth and clothed me with joy,
That my heart may sing your praises and not be silent.
Lord my God, I will praise you forever.
Psalm 30:4-5, 11-12

Anne Worth *has been in private practice for more than forty years. She specializes in addiction recovery, women's issues, faith exploration, and relationship enrichment. At the age of fifty-five, her life changed dramatically when she met Jesus. She readily shares the joy of her faith with everyone she meets. She rescues and fosters animals in need, serves homeless men and women at the Dallas Stewpot, and enjoys the privilege of being called Mama Anne by many in the Sudanese refugee community.*

Beliefs from God's Word

We believe . . . the Bible is the verbally inspired Word of God and without mistakes as originally written. It is the complete revelation of His will for salvation and the only unfailing rule of faith and practice for the Christian life.

We believe . . . in one God, Creator of all things, eternally existing in three persons: Father, Son, and Holy Spirit, and that these three are co-eternal and of equal dignity and power.

We believe . . . in the deity of Jesus Christ, His miraculous conception by the Holy Spirit, His virgin birth, His sinless life; His substitutionary death on a cross, His bodily resurrection, His ascension to the right hand of the Father, and His personal, imminent return.

We believe . . . that man was created by and for God. By man's disobeying God, every person incurred spiritual death, which is separation from God and physical death. All people are sinners by nature and practice.

We believe . . . the Lord Jesus Christ died for our sins, and all who believe in Him are declared righteous because of His sacrificial death and are, therefore, in right relationship with God.

We believe . . . in the present ministry of the Holy Spirit indwelling all believers and thus enabling and empowering the life and ministry of the believer.

We believe . . . in the bodily resurrection of everyone who has lived, the everlasting blessedness of those in right relationship with God, and the everlasting punishment of those who have rejected God's forgiveness in His Son.

God's Good News for You

Now that you have read these stories of great faith, you may want to know how you can have this same kind of faith. We have Good News for you.

He loves you!
For God so loved the world that he gave his one and only Son, that whoever believes in him shall not perish but have eternal life. — John 3:16

He wants to meet your need.
Your iniquities have separated you from your God; your sins have hidden his face from you, so that he will not hear. — Isaiah 59:2

God made him who had no sin to be sin for us, so that in him we might become the righteousness of God. — 2 Corinthians 5:21

He offers you a free gift!
The wages of sin is death, but the gift of God is eternal life in Christ Jesus our Lord. — Romans 6:23

How to receive this gift:
If you declare with your mouth, "Jesus is Lord," and believe in your heart that God raised him from the dead, you will be saved. — Romans 10:9

Jesus, I recognize I have sinned and need You. I believe You are the Son of God, that You died on the cross for my sin, rose from the dead and now sit at the right hand of God. I trust You alone and choose to follow You. Thank you for forgiving me of my sin and giving me eternal life. In Jesus' name, amen.

If you have chosen to receive God's gift or would like more information, please contact us at **info@RoaringLambs.org**. We would love to hear from you!

Share with Us

Roaring Lambs is working on our next volume of *Stories of Roaring Faith,* a book of testimonies designed to lead a nonbeliever to faith in Jesus Christ and to encourage the followers of Jesus. We would love to receive your testimony.

Please submit via email your typed, double-spaced, approximately 3,000-word story, as well as an 80- to 100-word bio. Include any contact information you want published.

Email: **info@RoaringLambs.org**

Website: **RoaringLambs.org/share-your-story**

In addition, you may be invited as a guest on our radio show, *A Time to Dream,* which also features life-changing testimonies.

Roaring Lambs is a 501(c)(3), which exists on tax deductible donations. We would welcome any gifts to sustain our ministry to equip believers to better communicate their faith. Donations may be made online at **RoaringLambs.org** or mailed to Roaring Lambs, 17110 Dallas Parkway, Suite 260, Dallas, TX 75248.

There are many ways to give to Roaring Lambs: check, credit card, gifts of stock or real estate, or planned gifts by will or trust. Roaring Lambs can help with any of the above by working with your attorney or accountant.

Give, and it will be given to you. A good measure, pressed down, shaken together and running over, will be poured into your lap. For with the measure you use, it will be measured to you. — Luke 6:38

About the Editors

Donna Skell

With a heart for God, people, and business, Donna stays active in the Christian community. She has been involved with this ministry since its inception and came on staff in 2008. Donna oversees all Roaring Lambs events and Bible studies. She co-hosts an international radio show called *A Time to Dream*, airing four times a week on three platforms. The program features powerful faith stories. By collecting these amazing stories, Roaring Lambs has produced four volumes of *Stories of Roaring Faith*. She especially enjoys speaking to ladies' groups, churches, and retreats. Her rich Jewish heritage and her study of God's Word enhance her insight into the issues involved in Christian faith and living. In addition to her work with Roaring Lambs, Donna serves on the Christian Women in Media Advisory Committee, and the Collin County Christian Prayer Breakfast Committee. **DSkell@RoaringLambs.org**

Belinda McBride

Answering God's call at the age of nine to become a "missionary," Belinda's mission was to touch others with the Good News of Jesus Christ. Her passion has been equipping believers to effectively live life with hope, purpose, and strength. She has done this as a pastor's daughter, pastor's wife, administrator, Bible study teacher, speaker, and writer.

She has served in many churches and ministries, including Hope for the Heart, Marketplace Ministries, and Roaring Lambs. Belinda's great joy is her husband, four daughters and fifteen grandchildren. She currently resides in Carrollton, Texas and is Director of Operations with Roaring Lambs. She can be contacted at **BMcBride@RoaringLambs.org**.

233

Lisa Burkhardt Worley

Lisa is an award-winning author and speaker, and is the Director of Special Projects for Roaring Lambs. She is also founder of "Pearls of Promise Ministries." Lisa has authored, co-authored, or co-edited nine books, *The Only Father I Ever Knew*, the *Pearls of Promise* devotional, *If I Only Had, The Most Powerful P: A Child's Introduction to the Power of Prayer, The Most Powerful P Activity Book and Prayer Journal,* and four volumes of *Stories of Roaring Faith.*

Lisa is a former television sportscaster, and now co-hosts an international weekly radio show with Donna Skell called, *A Time to Dream,* airing four times a week on three platforms. Lisa earned a Master of Theological Studies degree from Perkins School of Theology.

PearlsOfPromiseMinistries.com

Dr. Sherry Ryan

Dr. Ryan is a retired Associate Professor of Information Technology and Decision Sciences at the University of North Texas. She received her PhD in Information Systems from the University of Texas at Arlington and an MBA from the University of Southern California. Prior to earning her doctorate, she worked for IBM, teaching courses and speaking at national conferences.

She has published numerous academic journal articles, conference proceedings, and is currently working on a book. Sherry has two children, one granddaughter, and one grandson. She manages the Roaring Lambs website, is passionate about missions, and is on the Board of Directors for "His Appointed Time Ministries."

Ministry@RoaringLambs.org

Frank Ball

For ten years, Frank Ball directed North Texas Christian Writers to help members improve their writing and storytelling skills. In 2011, he founded Story Help Groups and joined the Roaring Writers ministry seven years later to encourage and equip all Christians to tell their life-changing stories. He has taught at writer's conferences and churches across the U.S. and Canada. Besides writing his own books, he does ghostwriting, copy editing, and graphic design to help others publish high-quality books.

As Pastor of Biblical Research and Writing for three years, he wrote sermons, teaching materials, and hundreds of devotions. He coaches writers, writes blogs, and is a panelist on The Writer's View. His first book, *Eyewitness: The Life of Christ Told in One Story*, is a compilation of biblical information on the life of Christ in a chronological story that reads like a novel. His website is **FrankBall.org**.

FBall@RoaringLambs.org

Made in the
USA
Lexington, KY